Julio Alberto Garibay Ruiz

Information Technology Convergence, Innovation Management and Firm Performance

Julio Alberto Garibay Ruiz

Information Technology Convergence, Innovation Management and Firm Performance

A Strategic Management Study in a Cross Order Region (San Diego, CA. U.S.A. - Baja California, Mexico)

VDM Verlag Dr. Müller

Imprint

Bibliographic information by the German National Library: The German National Library lists this publication at the German National Bibliography; detailed bibliographic information is available on the Internet at http://dnb.d-nb.de.

Cover image: www.purestockx.com

Publisher:
VDM Verlag Dr. Müller Aktiengesellschaft & Co. KG, Dudweiler Landstr. 125 a, 66123 Saarbrücken, Germany,
Phone +49 681 9100-698, Fax +49 681 9100-988,
Email: info@vdm-verlag.de

Produced in USA and UK by:
Lightning Source Inc., La Vergne, Tennessee, USA
Lightning Source UK Ltd., Milton Keynes, UK
BookSurge LLC, 5341 Dorchester Road, Suite 16, North Charleston, SC 29418, USA

ISBN: 978-3-639-06395-0

DEDICATION

This book is dedicated to my loving wife and friend, Veronica,

To my two sons, Jesus Adolfo and Angel Eduardo,

and to my parents, Adolfo and Maria de la Luz.

TABLE OF CONTENTS

Chapter   Page

Chapter   Page

LIST OF TABLES

LIST OF FIGURES

Chapter 1

THE RESEARCH PROBLEM

This is a strategic management research study that evaluated the information,

communications and entertainment convergence phenomenon and its relationships with new

service delivery strategies and operational capabilities that would be needed for enhanced

shareholder value creation and incremental overall firm performance. The objective of this

study was to examine certain characteristics of middle-level managers and corporate leaders

of high tech clusters in the cross-border region (San Diego, U.S. - Baja California, Mexico).

This chapter presents the background of the problem, the importance of information

technology convergence, the need to manage strategic innovation, a statement of the problem,

and the expected contributions to the academic field of strategic management and to the

practice of management.

The Scope of Convergence within This Study

Technological convergence is the process by which industries which were once

different in terms of their technological and therefore knowledge bases, come to share similar

technological and knowledge bases (Rosenberg, 1976). The convergence of computer and

1

telecommunication technology has led to the growing use of the expression "Information and Communication Technology (ICT)" to describe this transformation (Freeman and Soete, 2000: 160). A converged fixed and mobile service is one that enables the user to access a wide variety of communications, information, and/or entertainment services, with consistent quality of services regardless of the end terminal used, the underlying network over which those applications run, or the user's location (Gibson and Vestergaard, 2006).

General Background of the Problem

Table 1 shows that Schumpeter (1934, 1942) followed the Russian economist Kondratieff to describe waves of technical change as "successive industrial revolutions" in a historical-descriptive manner. According to Schumpeter, each business cycle was unique because of the variety of technical innovations; he saw innovation as the main engine of capitalist growth and the source of entrepreneurial profit (Freeman and Soete, 2000: 18-19).

Schumpeter was one of the first economists to define five possible types of innovation: (1) the introduction of a new product or a qualitative change in an existing product; (2) process innovation new to an industry; (3) the opening of a new market; (4) the development of new sources of supply for raw materials or other inputs; and (5) changes in industrial organization.

Table 1

Successive Waves of Technical Change

Approx. Timing	Kondratieff Waves	Science Technology Education and Training
First: 1780s –1840s	Industrial revolution: factory production for textiles	Apprenticeship learning by doing
Second: 1840s –1890s	Age of steam power and railways	Professional mechanical and civil engineers
Third: 1890s – 1940s	Age of electricity and steel	Industrial R&D labs, national and standards laboratories
Fourth: 1940s – 1990s	Age of mass production and synthetic materials	Large-scale industrial and government R&D
Fifth: 1990s – ?	Age of microelectronics and computer networks	R&D global networks, lifetime education and training

A simple definition of innovation is the sum of invention and exploitation. The invention process covers all efforts aimed at creating new ideas and getting them to work. The exploitation process includes all stages of commercial development, application and transfer, including the focusing of ideas or inventions toward specific objectives, evaluating those objectives, downstream transfer of research and/or development results, and the eventual broad-based utilization and diffusion of the technology-based outcomes (Roberts, 2007: 36).

The variety of innovations during the second wave of technical change includes the invention of the telephone by Alexander Graham Bell on March 10, 1876. He started a revolution in communications and commerce. This innovation spread a web of instantaneous information across towns, then a continent, then the world, and has greatly accelerated economic development. Some of the successive industrial revolutions were the first public demonstration in the U.S. of long-distance television transmission in 1937, when the Bell System sent live TV images of Herbert Hoover, then the Secretary of Commerce, over telephone lines from Washington, D.C. to an auditorium in Manhattan. Also, in 1939, Stibitz and S.B. Williams built the Complex Number Calculator, the world's first electrical digital computer. Its brain consisted of 450 telephone relays and 10 crossbar switches. Furthermore, a team including Alton Dickieson and D. Mitchell from Bell Labs and H.I. Romnes, worked more than a decade to complete the first mobile call in 1946. By 1948, wireless telephone service was available in almost 100 U.S. cities. The cellular telephone concept developed in 1947 by D. H. Ring at Bell Labs lay fallow until the 1960s, when Richard Frenkiel and Joel Engel of Bell Labs applied computers and electronics to make it work.

Considered the Magna Carta of communication, Shannon's Information Theory first appeared more than 50 years ago in his 1948 Bell System Technical Journal paper "The Mathematical Theory of Communication." Information Theory describes an ideal communications system in which all information sources—people speaking, computer keyboards, video cameras—have a "source rate" measured in bits per second (Shannon, 1993).

The transistor, more than any other single development, made possible the marriage of computers and communication. Three Bell Labs researchers—John Bardeen, William Shockley, and Walter Brattain—shared the Nobel Prize for their invention in 1947. In the years following its creation, the transistor gradually replaced the bulky, fragile vacuum tubes that had been used to amplify and switch signals. The transistor—and and eventually integrated circuits (microprocessors) that contained millions of transistors—served as the foundation for the development of modern electronics.

Gordon Moore, Intel co-founder, who published an article in Electronics magazine in 1965 in which he stated that innovations in technology would allow a doubling of the number of transistors in a given space every two years, and that the speed of those transistors would increase. (In 1964 he said the number would double annually, but later changed the interval to two years). The doubling of the number of transistors every two years became known as Moore's Law. Moore also stated that manufacturing costs would dramatically drop as the technology advanced. This scenario forecast silicon integration, which was made a reality by Intel, and has fueled the worldwide technology revolution.

The transistor was a revolutionary innovation because it destroyed the prior competence in vacuum tube technology. However, there is another category of innovations corresponding to Sahal's (1985) step-wise improvements in capabilities. These constitute nonrevolutionary discontinuities and are competence enhancing. Durand describes them as micro-radical innovations (Martin, 1994). For example, until the 1960s, voice communications between North America and the other continents was possible, but expensive. Then Bell Labs launched Echo, a giant, experimental balloon off of which messages could be bounced. Two years later Telstar was sent into orbit, the world's first active communications satellite.

In the mid-1970s, the U.S. Department of Defense (DOD) recognized an electronic communication problem developing within the organization. In the process of communicating the ever-increasing volume of electronic information among staff, research

5

labs, universities, and contractors, DOD had a hit a major obstacle. How could information be shared? The Advanced Research Projects Agency (ARPA) was assigned to resolve the problem of dealing with different networking equipment and topologies. ARPA formed an alliance with universities and computer manufacturers to develop communication standards. This alliance specified and built a four-node host network that is the foundation of today's Internet. During the 1970s, the network migrated to a new, core protocol design that became the basis for Transmit Control Protocol/Internet Protocol or TCP/IP (Ackermann et al., 1994). In 1977, a fiber optic communication system installation extending about 1.5 miles under downtown Chicago was the world's first light wave system to provide a full range of telecommunications services—voice, data, and video—over a public switched network.

The knowledge and information revolution began at the turn of the twentieth century and has gradually accelerated. By 1976 the number of white-collar workers employed in offices surpassed the number of farm workers, service workers, and blue-collar workers employed in manufacturing. Information technology is bringing about changes in organization that make the firm even more dependent than in the past on the knowledge, learning, and decision making of individual employees (Laudon and Laudon, 1998: 6-7).

While the introduction of the aforementioned micro-radical innovations follows an evolutionary process within the Schumpeter's industrial revolutions, the competitive landscape has been changing rapidly, especially since the AT&T divestiture ruling, by a U.S. Federal Court consent decree on December 31, 1983, that precipitated the separation of local and long distance telephone services. The next milestone was the Telecommunications Act

6

of 1996, which provided major changes in laws to stimulate competition in cable TV and on the Internet (Heldman, 1998: 3).

Furthermore, significant discontinuities such as globalization, deregulation, blurring of industry boundaries through new business models, technological convergence and disintermediation are posing new challenges and forcing managers to create new competencies (Prahalad, 1998). Indeed, the combination of the personal computer, the microprocessor, the Internet, and fiber optics fostered and demanded new business practices and types of skills which were less about the vertical chain of command for value creation and more about connecting and collaborating horizontally for value creation (Friedman, 2006: 208). Similarly, discontinuous technological innovations threaten the strategic position of many incumbents (Tushman and Anderson, 1986).

Technological innovations create new products based on new technological underpinnings. Over time, further developments improve the new technology's performance attributes in ways that mainstream customers value, to a point where the new technology begins to cannibalize the existing technology (Chistensen, 1997). New technologies also enable companies to create competitive advantage both in existing industries and in new, still unstructured industries. In addition, in a business environment characterized by rapid and disruptive technological changes, incumbents have to acquire new technological capabilities and explore new business opportunities in order to stay profitable in the long run (Vanhaverbeke and Peeters, 2005).

The components of the trio commonly called "triple play" today (voice, video, and data) were originally developed in different domains, and the networks carrying them were

7

designed and engineered specifically for their differing requirements. The implication was that different network environments had to be supported concurrently to allow all three services to exist (Rungta and Ben-Shalom, 2006). But convergence is a business issue, not only a technology issue, bundling alone will only shrink the customer's spending as value is eroded. Therefore, seamless blending of voice (wireline and wireless), data and video services is required to realize full converged revenue potential (Dial, 2006). The benefits of converged networks are clear. These architectures will enable carriers to increase revenue through enhanced services that adapt to customer demands and boost margins by reducing the cost of service delivery (Narayanaswamy and Dahr, 2002).

According to the Organization for Economic Co-operation and Development (OECD), commercial success and market forces will determine the direction which convergence takes and influence the environment within which policies must operate (Stretton, 2004). While carriers are expanding their activities by selling select mobile business applications, other members are also selling solutions to enterprise customers either directly or through other channels. VARs, system integrators, and hosted service providers, as well as middleware and database software vendors, and mobile application specialists all have different ways of going to market (Weldon, 2007).

There are two elements of support for organizations' future business strategy: The technology strategy and the societal strategy. Societal changes influence both the speed and impact of a new technology's introduction on the society. The societal changes in turn influence organizations' development of technology. Investment in technology is often translated into a short-term decrease in profits. Investors are resistant to decreases in profits, but without investment in technology, future profitability is threatened (Ansoff and Antoniou, 2004). Integration of these strategies is illustrated in Figure 1.

Figure 1

Integration of Business, Technology and Societal Strategies

The complexity in the socio-technological environment and the requirement for new technological capabilities to explore new business opportunities in order to stay profitable in the long-term often leads to creation of frameworks or models, whose main objective is the alignment of information technology with business goals. The Information Technology Infrastructure Library (ITIL) developed by the Office of Government Commerce in the U.K. is the most widely used best practice worldwide that specifically addresses the strategic business value generated by the IT organization and the need to deliver a high quality IT service. Using the broader library provides a comprehensive set of guidance to link the technical implementation with the strategic management of a modern business.

ITIL frequently is used in conjunction with other best-practice frameworks such as Control Objectives for Information and related Technology (COBIT), Capability Maturity Model Integration, and Six Sigma. Companies are free to mix and match these frameworks rather than choose one over the other. For example, ITIL processes support many of the objectives of COBIT, which was developed by the Information Systems Audit and Control Association and IT Governance Institute as a standard for IT security and control practices (Violino, 2005). Figure 2 shows a framework with the expected relationships among the socio-technological environment, business, information technology, strategy, and capabilities.

The business side of this model has been well developed, where levels of strategic aggressiveness and capability responsiveness appropriate to the level of environmental turbulence are required for business success. Significant gaps between appropriate and actual levels would indicate a firm that is poorly prepared to meet the future (Ansoff et al., 2004).

10

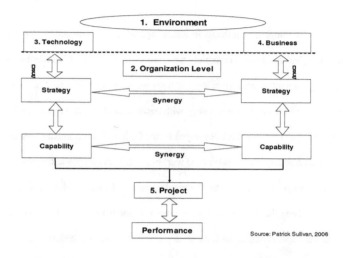

Figure 2

Environment, Business/Technology, Strategy and Capability Relationships

The technology side of the model has been developed through numerous studies that have examined the relationships between innovation and performance (Damanpour and Gopalakrishnan, 2001), empirical analysis between innovation and performance (Feeny and Rogers, 2003), how innovation within an organization can be measured and the results related to the organization's performance (Studt, 2005), innovation management for the business firm and society as a whole (Schumpeter, 1934), and so on. For the eight large world economic powers (the "Group of Eight", including: Canada, France, Germany, Italy, Japan, United Kingdom, United States, and Russia), these groundbreaking early contributions lay dormant for much of the post-World War II period. Organizations found little reason to

11

become systematic in innovation because there was little competition and ever-increasing demand. However, it was in the 1960s and 1970s when companies from Japan and newly industrialized countries captured large slices of market share in many important industries, that Western companies started to pay serious attention to innovation (Singh and Bernstein, 2006).

The Need for Research

The overall relationship between innovation and performance remains largely unclear (Subramanian and Nilakanta, 1996). To resolve the situation, substantial effort will need to be made to demonstrate the nature of the link between innovation management practices and organizational performance (Singh and Bernstein, 2006). Furthermore, Christensen's original theory focused on disruptive technologies. Over time, while the same theory has been used to explain all kinds of disruptive innovations, different kinds of innovations have different competitive effects and produce different kind of markets. They should be treated as distinct phenomena (Markides, 2006).

Basically, the same questions from ten years ago are addressed in this strategic management research: How much substance is behind the digital convergence hype? Are we on the verge of a true technological revolution that will reshape the global economy? What should companies and managers do to prepare for such a turbulent competitive environment? (Yoffie, 1997: 1). What kinds of models/channels target which customer segments? Are there too few options available or too many? Are these disparate solutions competitive or complementary, and how do they relate to carrier distribution models? (Weldon, 2007).

Therefore, further research is needed to analyze mechanisms of how Information Technology (IT) performance leads to overall performance and competitive advantage (Yum, 2000: 270), a need to research and improve the Ansoff Strategic Success Hypothesis, considering other dimensions of functional management capability or competitive responsiveness to improve upon the concept of integrative management (Gustafson, 2003: 263) and while the potential advantages of convergence are undisputed, they remain to be demonstrated in practice for most areas, and the promised economies and savings need to be documented (Fowler, 2005: 16).

Furthermore, R&D and market introduction methodologies that worked well within an existing paradigm, with relatively predictable cycles, are unlikely to work in highly turbulent environments. As a result, successful internal processes for the converging world will have to reflect at least two potentially conflicting imperatives: first, they have to be highly flexible and adaptive, and second, they must be very time-sensitive (Yoffie, 1997: 29).

Strategic Success Hypothesis and the Importance of Technology

While general management is responsible for the firm's strategic direction, it frequently fails to manage the organization's technological innovation process in both low and high technological industries (Ansoff, 1972). On one hand the focus of low technology organizations is primarily in utilizing and expanding technology innovation (Tellis and Golder, 2001). On the other, technology in high technology organizations is one of the critical determining factors of firms' future success (Kahaner, 1996). The following two theorems supporting paradigmic theory of strategic success behaviors of environment servicing organizations (ESOs) are used to improve the concept of integrative management (Ansoff et. al. 1993: 193).

Theorem 2.3 Strategic Success Formula - An ESO's performance is optimized whenever its Strategic Responsiveness (Strategic Aggressiveness plus Organizational Responsiveness) is aligned with the turbulence level of the ESO's environment.

Theorem 2.4 Importance of technology - In a technologically turbulent environment, the technological aggressiveness of an ESO is a major contributor to its success.

According to the Strategic Success Hypothesis, when environmental turbulence, strategic aggressiveness, and responsiveness of organizational capability are aligned in an

14

organization, performance is expected to be optimal (Ansoff and McDonnell, 1990).

Characteristics of the Strategic Success Hypothesis are described in Chapter 2A.

Statement of the Problem

This strategic management research study was concerned with empirical research that

relates environmental turbulence, information technology convergence, strategic innovation

management and performance on Technology Convergence Issues. The study hypothesized

that when environmental turbulence associated with technological issues, innovative service

delivery strategies implemented through strategic aggressiveness, and required

responsiveness of organizational capability are aligned in an organization, performance on

convergence issues is expected to be optimal. The focus of the study was on high tech

clusters in the cross-border region (San Diego, U.S. - Baja California, Mexico), the

technological-innovation differences between middle-level managers and corporate leaders,

and thus performance on convergence issues differs in the two countries. Finally, the study

addressed the organization's technology convergence innovation process in both low and

high technological industries; hypothesized that the focus of low technology organizations is

primarily in utilizing and expanding technology convergence innovation, and that technology

convergence in high technology organizations is one of the critical determining factors of

firms' future success.

15

Contributions to the Academic Field of Strategic Management

The expected contributions of this study from an academic perspective were to provide empirical evidence about the relationships among environmental turbulence associated with technological issues, innovative service delivery strategies implemented through strategic aggressiveness, required responsiveness of organizational capability and performance on Technology Convergence Issues.

Contributions to the Practice of Management

The expected contributions and application to the practice of management focused on the appropriate use of technology convergence strategies in low and high technology organizations in the cross-border region (San Diego, U.S. - Baja California, Mexico) and on measures to help managers identify convergence drivers for firms' future success.

Summary

The purpose of Chapter 1 is to present the research problem involving the phenomenon of convergence of information, communications and entertainment and its relationships with new service delivery strategies and operational capabilities that would be needed for enhanced shareholder value creation and incremental profitable revenue growth. The expected contributions to the academic field of strategic management were to provide

16

empirical evidence about the relationships among environmental turbulence associated with technological issues, innovative service delivery strategies implemented through strategic aggressiveness, required responsiveness of organizational capability and performance on convergence issues. The application to the practice of management is to focus on the appropriate use of technology convergence strategies in low and high technology organizations in the cross-border region (San Diego, U.S. - Baja California, Mexico) and to help managers identify convergence drivers for firms' future success.

Definitions

This section provides definitions of important terms used in this study:

Capability (firms' or managers') motivation, competence, capacity to manage change.

Capacity or bandwidth is defined as the channel through which the source's data travels as measured in bits per second. Information can be transmitted only if the source rate does not exceed the channel's maximum capacity, now known as the Shannon limit (Shannon, 1993).

Capacity is part of the capability vector: the volume of work which can be handled by an organizational unit of time.

Data, in computing, is information that has been translated into a form that is more convenient to move or process. Relative to today's computers and transmission media, data is information converted into binary digital form.

17

Information is stimuli that have meaning in some context for its receiver. When information is entered into and stored in a computer, it is generally referred to as data. After processing (such as formatting and printing), output data can again be perceived as information. When information is packaged or used for understanding or doing something, it is known as knowledge.

Information Technology (IT) encompasses all forms of technology used to create, store, exchange, and use information in its various forms (business data, voice conversations, still images, motion pictures, multimedia presentations, and other forms, including those not yet conceived). It's a term for including both telephony and computer technology in the same word. It is the technology that is driving what has often been called "the information revolution."

Host network The four nodes making up the network implemented in 1969 through 50 Kbps lines were UCLA (University of California Los Angeles), SRI (Stanford Research Institute), UCSB (University of California Santa Barbara), and The University of Utah. (http://www.zakon.org/robert/internet/timeline/).

Laser Almost all modern communications, including everything from cable television to the Internet, are carried on digital pulses of focused, high-intensity light called "lasers." The laser coupled with transmission lines of hair-thin, super-transparent, ultra-strong glass fiber today carry tens of billions of "bits" of information.

18

Modem is defined as a device used to convert digital data from the terminal or personal

computer into analog data for transmission over the dial-up phone copper network and vice

versa, where the transmission rate in bits per second (bps) is equal to the number of signaling

events per second (baud rate). For example, if the baud rate of a modem is 2400 signaling

events per second and the modem is able to interpret two bits per signaling event, then the

transmission speed is 4800 bps (Goldman, 1998).

Strategic aggressiveness as described by Ansoff and McDonnell (1990: 32) has two

characteristics:

1. The degree of discontinuity from the past of the firm's new product/services,

    competitive environments, and marketing strategies.

2. Timeliness of introduction of the firm's new products/services relative to new

    products/services which have appeared in the market.

Strategic capability of a firm was defined by Ansoff and McDonnell (1990: 262) as "its

propensity and its ability to engage in behavior which will optimize attainment of the form's

near-and long-term objectives."

Strategic Management A process for managing a firm's relationship with its environment. It

consists of strategic planning, capability planning, and management of change.

Switched or dial-up line is defined as POTS or "plain old telephone service." More formally,

the phone network is referred to as the public switched telephone network. Calls placed over

dial-up lines through Central Offices (CO) switches to modems (modulators/demodulators) that have connections built from available circuits are called circuit-switched-modem connections (Goldman, 1998).

Technology, types of

- **Fertile** A technology characterized by frequent product innovations.
- **Stable** A technology which remains unchanged from inception to the maturity stage of a demand life cycle.
- **Turbulent** A technology whose life cycle is short relative to the length of the demand life cycle.

Turbulence is defined as changeability in an environment characterized by the degree of novelty of challenges and the speed with which they develop.

Chapter 2A

GENERAL THEORETICAL FRAMEWORK

The related research topics in this and the following chapter are divided into two parts. The first part, Chapter 2A, is the conceptual design of the global model of all variables and relationships depicted in the model and a narrative discussion of the flow through the model. The second part, Chapter 2B, is the conceptual design of the research model that is a section of the global model studied. It includes a review of literature in support of the research questions that address the problem, the research hypotheses and variable names, and conceptual and operational definitions.

<u>Global Model</u>

The global model is based on the environment, business/technology, strategy and capability relationships framework depicted in Chapter 1, Figure 2 and includes the total reality surrounding the research problem to be described in Chapter 2B. The global model shown in Figure 3 is divided into four sections: the top section, labeled (1) and further depicted in Figure 4, encompasses environmental and Information Technology turbulences and their interactions with the firm.

21

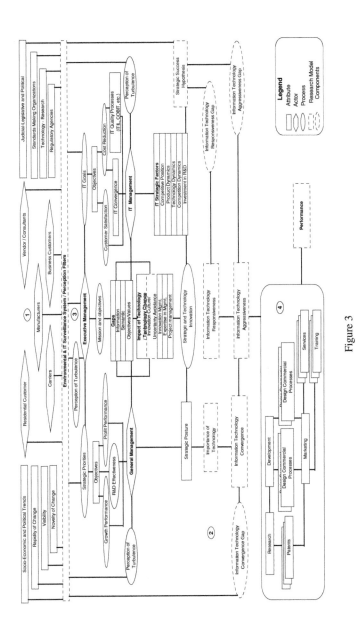

Figure 3

The Global Model

22

The second section, below, labeled (2) and shown in Figure 5, contains business-technology strategies, synergies and the relationships with the external environmental and IT turbulences. The next section, labeled (3) and further depicted in Figure 6, shows the strategic business, technological capabilities and their synergies through the Strategic Success Hypothesis and the importance of technology (Theorem 2.4). The bottom section, labeled (4) and depicted in Figure 7, shows downstream coupling and interactions with business and technological areas.

Literature to Support the Global Model

The following paragraphs present the relevant literature review, along with graphic and narrative descriptions of the variables and relationships described in the global model. The discussion is divided according to the four sub-sections of the global model: (1) the environmental and IT turbulences and their interactions with the firm; (2) the business-technology strategy synergies and their relationships with the firm; (3) strategic business and technological alignment; and (4) downstream coupling of strategic and technological innovation.

Environmental and Information Technology Turbulences

The IT industry today consists of a rapidly evolving and massively interconnected network of organizations, technologies, products, and consumers. In contrast with the vertically integrated environment of the 1960s and 1970s, today's industry is divided into a

large number of segments producing specialized components, systems and services. The IT

industry began the 21st century by entering a deep recession, exacerbated by excessive

investment and business failures in the Internet, software, and telecommunications industries.

Since the period of retrenchment, the IT industry has regained its health, rebounding from its

recession and delivering significant levels of innovation (Iansiti and Richards, 2006). The

data communications environment is the sum total of the interacting components, including

Judicial, political/legislative, standards making organizations, technology/research,

regulatory agencies, business customers, residential customers, manufacturers, carriers,

vendors and consultants. There is no distinct beginning or end. No one component is more

important than another (Goldman, 1998: 5). The external and IT environments and the

interactions with the firm are shown in Figure 4.

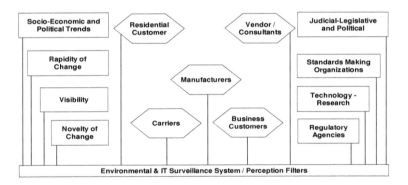

Figure 4

External and IT Environment and the Interactions with the Firm

24

In defining environmental turbulence, Ansoff and McDonnell (1990) were influenced by three sources. One was Alfred D. Chandler, whose findings that the strategy/capability transformation process was triggered by an environmental discontinuity and that firms regained their profitability only when their strategy and capability were aligned with the new state of their environment. Another source was a seminal paper by F.E. Emery and E.L. Trist that proposed a taxonomy of observable environments which are discrete and different from one another. The third source was Niels Bohr's model of the atom, in which turbulence was described in terms of a 5-point scale of discrete orbits named turbulence levels (Bedeian, 1992: 19). This scale is illustrated in Table 2.

Table 2

Levels of Environmental Turbulence

| Turbulence Characteristic | Turbulence Level | | | | |
	1 Repetitive	2 Expanding	3 Changing	4 Discontinuous	5 Surprising
Complexity	National	+	Regional	+	Global
Familiarity of events	Familiar	Extrapolable		Discontinuous familiar	Discontinuous novel
Rapidity of Change	Slower than response		Comparable to response		Faster than response
Visibility of Future	Recurring	Forecastable	Predictable	Partially predictable	Unpredictable surprises

As Table 2 shows, the respective levels of turbulence are described as a combined measure of the discontinuity or changeability, predictability, and frequency of the shifts of the firm's environment. Changeability is composed of the complexity and relative novelty of the successive challenges which the firm encounters in the environment. Predictability is the ratio of the speed with which challenges evolve in the environment to the speed of the firm's response (rapidity of change). Another factor is the visibility of the future which refers to the adequacy and the timeliness of information about the future (Ansoff and McDonnell, 1990: 31).

At the lowest turbulence level of 1, the business environment is a placid one in which a firm can confine its attention to its historical marketplace, successive challenges are a repetition of the past, change is slower than the firm's ability to respond and the future is expected to replicate the past. At 5, the highest turbulence level, a small (but growing) and important group of industries are of the creators of economic and technological progress. These are the high tech industries, born of novel technologies. These are also new industries in the burgeoning service sector. Their challenge is to use leading edge technologies to create products which serve previously unfilled needs of society, and thus create new industries (Ansoff and McDonnell, 1990).

The Business - Technology Strategy Synergies

According to Ansoff's Strategic Success Hypothesis, when environmental turbulence, strategic aggressiveness, and responsiveness of organizational capability are aligned in an

26

organization, performance is expected to be optimal (Ansoff and McDonnell, 1990).

Furthermore, as previously stated in Theorem 2.4 - Importance of Technology; in a

technologically turbulent environment, the technological aggressiveness of an environment

serving organization (ESO) is a major contributor to its success. Figure 5 shows the

relationships among characteristics of the Strategic Success Hypothesis, the importance of

technology theorem and the business-technology strategy synergies with the firm.

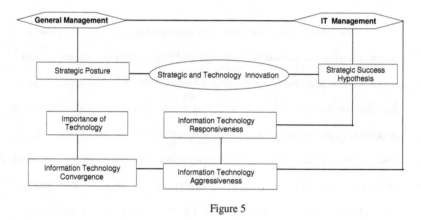

Figure 5

The Business-Technology Strategy Synergies

Ansoff and McDonnell (1990) borrowed the organization environment-matching

concept from the requisite variety theorem by W. R. Ashby. This theorem states that in order

to succeed in its environment, an organization must match the complexity of its response to

the complexity of the environment. In translating Ashby's theorem into strategic

management terminology, Ansoff equated Ashby's concept of environmental complexity with the concept of environmental turbulence, and the concept of organizational complexity with the combination of strategic aggressiveness and organizational responsiveness. The concept of strategic aggressiveness is measured by two characteristics: discontinuity of a firm's consecutive strategic moves in its environment, and timing of the firm's strategic moves relative to the moves of competitors in its environment. Table 3 shows the characteristics of strategic aggressiveness that match the 5-point scale of discrete turbulence environmental levels.

Table 3

Strategic Aggressiveness versus Environmental Turbulence

Turbulence Characteristic	Turbulence Level				
	1	2	3	4	5
	Repetitive	Expanding	Changing	Discontinuous	Surprising
Strategic aggressiveness	Stable, based on precedents	Reactive incremental, based on experience	Anticipatory incremental, based on extrapolation	Entrepreneurial discontinuous, based on expected futures	Creative discontinuous based on creativity

For measuring capability, Ansoff and McDonnell (1990) used organizational responsiveness measured by the openness of an organization to its environment, and by the way the organization handles change. Table 4 shows the characteristics of responsiveness of organizational capability that match the 5-point scale of discrete turbulence environmental levels.

28

Table 4

Responsiveness of Organizational Capability versus Environmental Turbulence

	Turbulence Level				
Turbulence Characteristic	1 Repetitive	2 Expanding	3 Changing	4 Discontinuous	5 Surprising
Responsiveness Of organizational capability	Custodial	Production	Marketing	Strategic	Flexible
	Precedent-driven	Efficiency-Driven	Market-driven	Environment-driven	Seeks to create environment
	Suppresses Change	Adapts to change	Seeks familiar change	Seeks new change	Seeks novel change
	Seeks stability ◄— Seeks		operating	efficiency —►	Seeks creativity
			◄— Seeks	strategic	efficiency —►
	Closed system	◄————————————————————►			Open system

Strategic Business and Technological Alignment

The resource-based view of the firm conceptualizes a firm as a bundle of resources and considers it as the basis for a firm's competitive position (Wernerfelt, 1984). The knowledge-based perspective of the firm postulates that knowledge assets produce long-term benefits such as competitive advantage and sustainability in the face of a fluctuating economic climate (Cole, 1998; Nonaka and Takeuchi, 1995; Spender, 1996). Knowledge integration is a focal aspect of the knowledge-based theory of the firm for application to tasks as well as for creation of new knowledge (Grant, 1996). Furthermore, IT plays an important

29

role in the firm's ability to apply existing knowledge effectively and to create new knowledge (Alavi and Leidner, 2001).

The concern with the process by which individuals acquire knowledge and understanding of their world traces back to antiquity. The Greeks called this concern the problem of epistemology (Ansoff, 1987). Although the study of knowledge has its roots in antiquity, the field of Knowledge Management (KM) as a self-conscious discipline is a recent phenomenon (Grossman, 2006). Peter Drucker (1994) was one of the first management gurus to laud the centrality of knowledge in the organizational context, stressing that the collective knowledge residing in the minds of its employees, customers, suppliers, and so on, is the most vital resource for an organization's economic growth, even more than the traditional factors of production (land, labor and capital).

Knowledge Management is evolving into a strategically important area for most organizations. Broadly, KM can be viewed as the process by which organizations leverage and extract value from their intellectual or knowledge assets. Knowledge has been described as information combined with experience, context, interpretation, and reflection (Davenport, 1993).

A number of KM processes and mechanisms can be used to facilitate knowledge integration across business and IT. Two such processes are the participation of IT managers in business planning and of business managers in strategic IT planning (Keams and Lederer, 2003). Within the context of strategic IT planning, knowledge integration relates to the integration of business and IT knowledge. An important outcome of this knowledge integration is greater linkage of the strategic IT plan to business goals and objectives with the focus on the extent to which the strategic IT plan is aligned with the business strategy. Thus, it can be argued that knowledge context facilitates sharing of domain knowledge (the knowledge integration process), which in turn, affects knowledge integration outcomes (Reich and Benbasat, 1996, 2000 and Sabherwal, 1999).

The strategic alignment of business and IT in the global model and its relationship with the environment have been distributed among three main components: Executive or top managers' knowledge of IT, general or business managers' participation in strategic IT, and IT managers' participation in business planning. As adapted from Ansoff and McDonnell (1990), executive management is understood to be in charge of management of growth, diversification and acquisition; general management integrates, coordinates and directs functional or IT management efforts toward common goals, and functional or IT management is in charge of R&D, innovation, project management, training and services. The strategic alignment between business and IT is shown in Figure 6.

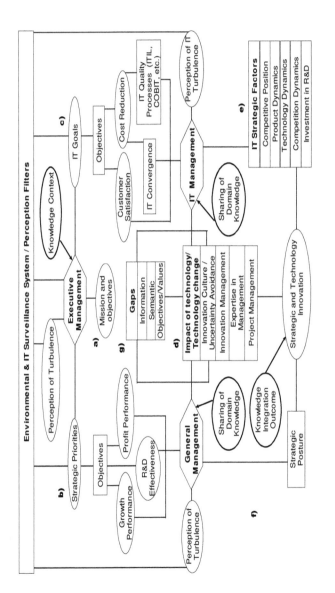

Figure 6

Strategic Alignment Between Business and IT

32

The success of today's enterprises, measured in terms of growth and profit performance, is highly dependent on the inner workings and capabilities of their IT function. Consequently, today's IT function is driven by the very same dynamics as the enterprise itself (Krafzig et al., 2004). The following paragraphs address, on both business and IT managerial levels, some of the functions considered in this study to foster and achieve strategic alignment between business and IT. These paragraphs expand upon the items in Figure 6 designated with the letters a) through g).

a) Mission and Objectives

The mission of the firm is the list of aspirations of the influential constituencies (commonly called stakeholders in the U.S.) which the firm serves. Once the mission is formulated, the second step is to translate the mission into criteria which management can use for guiding the firm's performance. The results of this translation are the goals and objectives of the firm (Ansoff et al., 1993: 122).

b) Strategic Priorities (Objectives)

The strategic priorities originate from the firm's vision and mission. As the business environment changes, strategic priorities will change. It is common practice in business firms to state two performance objectives: Growth performance is typically expressed as the future annual percentage growth rate of sales, and profit performance is expressed in terms of the net profit ratio to the equity investment as the profitability goal (Ansoff et al., 1993: 123). A third objective would be the measurement of R&D effectiveness in terms of numbers of patents, numbers of innovations, and so on (Freeman and Soete, 2000: 112).

33

c) IT Goals

Goal setting is a key step to ensure that IT goals are aligned with the firm's mission, objectives and strategic priorities. Enterprises are working to become more "transparent," making possible: greater "visibility" into business processes, greater flexibility and manageability, seamless interoperability with business partners and a focus on core competencies. The increased visibility into business process also makes possible better customer service and real-time collaboration with both customers and business partners. In addition, transparency provides the fundamentals for good enterprise risk management and makes compliance with regulations easier. Innovative uses of emerging technologies such a Component Business Modeling (CBM) and Services Oriented Architectures (SOA), coupled with an increased number of industry-specific standards, are delivering the tools and methods to bridge business and IT more easily and efficiently (Von Kanel, 2006). The Information Technology Infrastructure Library (ITIL) and Control Objectives for Information and related Technology (CobIT) are examples of industry-specific standards.

d) Impact of Technology and Technology Change

The impact of technology depends on the technological turbulence of the environment. The general management capability components that are impacted by technological variables such as product life cycles and rate of technological change are: Involvement in innovation management, expertise in management of technology, innovative culture, firm flexibility, project management, strategic control, technological information systems and budgeting for innovation (Ansoff and McDonnell, 1990: 190).

34

Innovative culture is addressed from a cross-cultural dimension. Although other theories of cultural differences exist (Triandis, 1993), Hofstede's dimensions are the most influential framework for comparing cultures (Hanges et al., 1997). To understand cultural differences between countries, Hofstede developed four dimensions to categorize values and norms (Hofstede, 1990): Power distance, uncertainty avoidance, individualism-collectivism, and masculinity-femininity.

To help us understand cultural differences between the U.S. and Mexico, Hofstede (1980) describes the U.S. as a small power distance culture that emphasizes interdependence and fewer hierarchical organizational structures with a preference for democratic and consultative decision-making styles. In contrast, Mexico is a large power distance culture; emphasizes dependence within hierarchical organizational structures; and prefers autocratic, directive and centralized decision-making styles. The U.S. is characterized as having weak uncertainty avoidance, which implies less resistance to change, a willingness to take risks, less acceptance of rules and regulations, and a view of conflict as natural and inevitable. Alternatively, Mexico, on the other hand, is characterized as having strong uncertainty avoidance, value conservatism, risk avoidance, security, and law and order through written rules and regulations. The U.S. also demonstrates high individualism and self-orientation which value individual autonomy, initiative, pleasure, security, and decision making. In contrast, Mexico exhibits low individualism, a more collective orientation that emphasizes the importance of expertise, order, and group decision making to support the interests of one's in-group.

Mexico is characterized, in Hofstede's dimensions, as a high collectivist culture, with high power distance and high uncertainty avoidance, qualities which reduce the success of

35

projects such as standard online design mechanisms. Discussion boards, scheduled chats and weekly deliverables have typically succeeded in U.S. culture (Kumar and Kelly, 2006). According to Kumar and Kelly, the role of the manager or supervisor is very important to Mexicans for problem solving, due to the higher power distance. Furthermore, uncertainty avoidance is very relevant to technology skills transfer work in Mexico. Students found open-ended interaction with entrepreneurs very difficult to manage and actually avoided interacting with the business owners as a way to minimize the uncertainty of their task. While Mexican students had difficulty developing a sense of being part of an in-group when course work was delivered online, due to their collectivist culture, their productivity increased when they had face-to-face meetings with the researchers and group leaders.

It is commonplace in the knowledge management literature to read about the all-important linkage between knowledge management and competitive advantage without concepts for handling cross-cultural factors. It seems that experts on knowledge management are as yet unclear about how to handle cross-cultural phenomena; and that experts on culture and cross-cultural issues have yet to contemplate culture as a form of knowledge and from there to treat culture as an organizational resource and accordingly as an object of knowledge management (Holden, 2001).

One of the technological characteristics of environment that impact general management capability is the rate of technological change. Organizational revolution is multi-faceted and involves technological change, international trade, and so on. It is propelled, in large part, by advances in computer and telecommunication technologies in conjunction with corresponding human skills, transforming the flow of information in modern economies. A major implication of this transformation is that it calls for new forms of organizing economic activity and these, in turn, appear to be exerting a major influence by reversing the labor mix from one engineer – 5 technicians – 50 craftsmen during the era of the Industrial Revolution to a new proportion – 50 engineers – 10 technicians – 5 craftsmen, during the present regime of the Organizational Revolution, which relies heavily on fast dissemination of sophisticated technical knowledge (Swamy, 2005).

Wernerfelt (1984) conceptualizes the resource-based view of the firm as a bundle of resources and considers it as the basis for a firm's competitive position. A firm's ability to manage its knowledge-based resource capabilities has become increasingly important as a result of performance threats triggered by technology change (Carrillo and Gaimon, 2004).

Managing the innovation of complex technologies requires operating in an ever-more dynamic and uncertain environment. In this environment, innovation networks are replacing the individual firm as the focus of management. Thus, management is as much about identifying and helping to put into place organizational change as it is about facilitating technological change. Innovating network organizational processes that identify, access and coordinate changing arrays of strategically important knowledge resources has now become critical (Kash and Rycroft, 2003).

Information Technology managers experience problems due to change, and apply coping mechanisms both reactively and proactively to address them. For example, they reactively rely on vendors to resolve problems with new products after they occur. Also, they proactively work with vendors to improve future versions of IT (Benamati et al., 1997). Lavie (2006) integrates substitution and evolution capabilities as the extremes, and capability transformation as a third mechanism resting at an intermediate point along the continuum.

Among the eight large world economic powers (the "Group of Eight," including: Canada, France, Germany, Italy, Japan, United Kingdom, United States, and Russia), the three methods for managing discontinuous change (coercive, adaptive and crisis response) follow a serial problem-solving paradigm which was developed by the rationalist philosophers and, in particular, by Descartes. Concern with implementation should be delayed until after planning has been completed. A parallel approach, "the accordion method," permits management to expand or contract the duration of the change in response to the urgency dictated by the environment (Ansoff and McDonnell, 1990).

Findings related to the implementation of technological change suggest that the adoption of technological changes by individuals is largely based on their perceptions of how the technology will impact their jobs. Consequently, it appears that individuals who perceive that technology changes will improve their ability to perform their job tasks may be more willing to adopt the technology (Schraeder et al., 2006).

e) IT Strategic Factors

Ansoff and Antoniou (2004) discussed six variables that influence an organization's development and direction: Competitive position, power center, technological progress, type of technology cycle, product life cycle, and competitive dynamics. The competitive position it helps assess an organization's future competitive position in the market. The firm's competitive position role can be imitator, follower or leader.

Technological progress assesses the competitive dynamics of technology through technological product differentiation, use of technology as a competitive tool, and the technology intensity of the market. The technology cycle determines the length and frequency of introduction of new technologies to the market, and the number of competing technologies. There are two types of technology cycles in turbulent environments: fertile and turbulent. Fertile life cycles exist when the basic technology is long lived within the demand life cycle and products proliferate offering incrementally better performance. Turbulent cycles require the invention of new technologies that replace the new ones.

f) Perception of Turbulence and Strategic Posture

Past research has assumed that decision makers accurately perceive environmental issues and formulate their strategies based on their own perceptions (Sutcliffe, 1994). Individual judgments and perceptions of the involved managers are highly influenced by their personal strategic culture, personality, mindset, and prior experiences (Ansoff and McDonnell, 1990).

Strategic planning does not necessarily expect the future to be an improvement over the past, nor is it assumed to be extrapolable. A firm's prospects are made through an analysis of threats, trends and opportunities, which may change the historical trends. Strategic posture management is composed of strategic planning, capability planning, and systematic management of the resistance to change during implementation of the strategy and capability plans (Ansoff and McDonnell, 1990).

g) Gaps Between General Managers and Technologists

While the process of introducing IT into work organizations warrants an integrated perspective on economic, technical, human and organizational aspects of IT, it appears that technical and economic considerations dominate the practitioner landscape. Paradoxically, when IT fails to deliver, as it so often does, human and organizational considerations are the prime determinants of such underperformance and failure. This poses an intractable dilemma for many organizations. The dilemma is of an enduring nature, sustained by the behavioral patterns of polarized occupational groups who have vested, but divergent, interests in exploiting IT. Executive management tends to view the introduction of IT as an economic imperative while IT specialists tend to view it as a technical imperative. The coalescent nature of these two imperatives is such that human and organizational considerations are regularly marginalized and ignored during the process of introducing IT into work organizations (McDonagh and Coghlan, 2006).

There are three typical gaps confronted between general managers and technologists in turbulent, technology-intensive industries: (1) The information gap, in which knowledge workers are kept from contact with the strategists by several intervening layers of managers, who have neither competence nor interest in technology, and who suppress and filter technological information; (2) the semantic gap, based on differences in language, concepts,

40

and perception of success factors between the general managers and the R&D managers; (3) the objectives/value gap, in which, for the technologist, a technologically feasible advance is reason enough to go to market, while the general managers need to be convinced of its potential profitability (Ansoff and McDonnell, 1990).

Downstream Coupling of Strategic and Technological Innovation

When the firm makes a large investment in the innovation process the nature of the organizational capability will differ significantly, depending on the relative importance of R&D investment (Ansoff and McDonnell, 1990: 183). Simply to commit greater resources to R&D does not guarantee successful innovation and could lead to lower growth through a so-called "business stealing effect" based on Schumpetarian features of "creative destruction" (Freeman and Soete, 2000: 303 and 328).

Almost all case studies of the management of innovation in Western Europe and the United States point to the lack of integration between R&D, production management and marketing as a major source of failure (Freeman and Soete, 2000: 149). To increase efficiencies and maximize shareholder profit, today's managers are looking for IT-based tools and techniques to improve performance (Mamaghani, 2006). According to a 2005 study by Bain & Company, the top four tools used by today's managers are strategic planning, customer relationship management, benchmarking and outsourcing. The Knowledge Management tool is one used as an average by today's managers (Rigby, 2005).

Five critical behavioral functions are identified within the technology-based innovation activities in an R&D project. These functions are idea generating, entrepreneurship or championing, project leading, gatekeeping, and sponsoring or coaching. Some unique individuals are able to perform concurrently more than one of the critical roles. Each type must be recruited, managed and supported differently, offered different sets of incentives, and supervised with different types of measures and controls. Organizations have failed to be innovative solely because one or more of these five critical roles has been absent (Roberts and Fusfeld, 1982). Figure 7 depicts the downstream coupling of strategic and technological innovation.

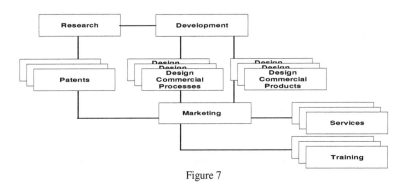

Figure 7

Downstream Coupling of Strategic and Technological Innovation

Summary

Chapter 2A contains the conceptual design of the global model of all variables and relationships to be depicted in the research model, and a narrative discussion of the flow through the model. The primary frameworks under which the global model was designed are the integration of business, technology and societal strategies (Figure 1) and environment, business/technology, strategy and capability relationships (Figure 2).

The global model is divided into four sub-sections with graphic and narrative descriptions of the variables and relationships: (1) the environmental and IT turbulences and their interactions with the firm; (2) the business-technology strategy synergies and relationships with the firm; (3) strategic business and technological alignment; and (4) downstream coupling of strategic and technological innovation.

The business-technology strategy synergies and relationships with the firm are based on the levels of environmental turbulence and strategic aggressiveness compared to environmental turbulence and responsiveness of organizational capability as compared to environmental turbulence.

Strategic business and technological alignment applies relevant insights from the knowledge-based theory and the resource-based view of the firm to the conduct of research through Knowledge Management processes, mechanisms and strategic dimensions of technology, for the purpose of facilitating knowledge integration across business and Information Technology.

Chapter 2B

RESEARCH MODEL AND SUPPORTING LITERATURE

This chapter presents the research model and the literature relevant to support the section of the global model studied. It describes the research questions, hypotheses, and variable names, presents conceptual definitions and operational definitions, and provides a chapter summary.

The primary framework under which this study was conducted is based on Ansoff's Strategic Success Hypothesis (Ansoff and McDonnell, 1990). However, this study also focused on relevant insights from the knowledge-based theory and the resource-based view of the firm to conduct research through Knowledge Management (KM) processes, mechanisms and strategic dimensions of technology that can be used to facilitate knowledge integration across business and Information Technology.

Research Model

The section of the global model studied follows Ansoff's Strategic Success Hypothesis in terms of strategic dimensions of Information Technology. The research model depicted in Figure 8 shows a mechanism of how convergence could lead to the improved

Performance on Information Technology Convergence Issues and competitive advantage and how it could improve and complement the Strategic Success Hypothesis, considering other dimensions of IT responsiveness or technology aggressiveness to improve upon the concept of integrative management. That is, a firm's Performance on Information Technology Convergence Issues will be optimal when the information technology aggressiveness of the firm's strategic behavior matches the turbulence of its technological environment, the responsiveness of the firm's technology capability matches the aggressiveness of its strategy and the components of the firm's technology capability are supportive of one another.

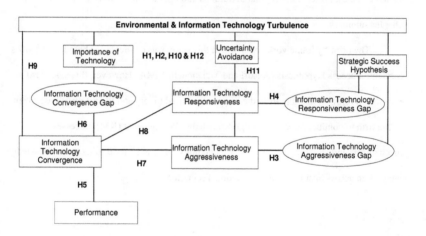

Figure 8

The Research Model

45

Research Variables

This section provides a review of the relevant literature of the conceptual definitions and operational definitions for the variables in the research model.

Information Technology Turbulence

The main characteristics of IT turbulence as used in this study are based on the environmental turbulence of the Strategic Success Hypothesis presented in Chapter 2A (Ansoff and McDonnell, 1990). To complement those characteristics, De Luca and Atuagene-Gima (2007) discussed environmental turbulence and technological uncertainty characteristics based on Jaworski and Kohli (1993) elements to describe the market and competitive environment, where technological uncertainty reflects the speed of change and instability of the technology environment, and environmental turbulence reflects rapid market and technological changes that managers perceive as hostile and stressful conditions for their firm. Turbulence often renders current firms' competencies obsolete (Tushman and Nelson, 1990), leading managers to upgrade existing capabilities and develop entirely new ones (Day, 1994). The elements included in their studies are summarized below:

- The actions of local and foreign competitors in our markets were changing quite rapidly
- Technological changes in our industry were rapid and unpredictable
- The market competitive conditions were highly unpredictable

46

- Customers' product preferences changed quite rapidly

- Changes in customers' needs were quite unpredictable

- It was very difficult to forecast technology developments in our industry

- Technology environment was highly uncertain

- Technological developments were highly unpredictable

- Technologically, our industry was a very complex environment

To understand environmental turbulence from the cross-border perspective, some of the export-oriented manufacturing and regional trade agreements are discussed here. Mexico's experience with the so-called "maquiladora corporations" (generally, direct subsidiaries of transnational firms) goes back to 1965, when they were set up along the border areas in cooperation with the American government to discourage illegal migration while protecting domestic manufacturers (Cooney, 2001). Under this arrangement, imports of raw materials and parts from the U.S. were allowed into Mexico without duties or restrictions on the condition that the finished goods were sent back to the U.S. with taxes paid only on the value added by the Mexican workers (Werlin, 2004).

Over the last 20 years, each side of the San Diego-Baja California border region has added more than 100,000 jobs in what are considered high value-added, globally competitive clusters; both sides have significantly expanded research institutes and higher education institutions and both enjoy a level of prosperity that exceeds that of other regions in Mexico and United States (Owens and Walshok, 2005: 4).

The North American Free Trade Agreement (NAFTA), a regional trade agreement between the U.S., Canada and Mexico, was implemented in 1994. Many in the U.S. were

47

concerned that the elimination of trade barriers would allow firms to move to Mexico to take advantage of their relatively cheap labor, which would result in diminished production and employment in the U.S. Also, the concern with greater environmental regulations in the U.S. was that the cost of domestic production would rise. This would encourage firms to move their production to other countries with relatively lax regulations and, in turn, cheaper production costs (MacDermott, 2006).

Information Technology Aggressiveness

This section focuses on the characteristics of Information Technology Aggressiveness. These characteristics are based on the Strategic Success Hypothesis and Table 3 presented in Chapter 2A. This section also drew on technological success factors discussed by Ansoff and McDonnell (1990) to determine the future environmental turbulence, the technological aggressiveness of a firm's strategy, the gaps and the action priorities of the firm.

The concept of strategic aggressiveness is measured by two characteristics: discontinuity of a firm's consecutive strategic moves in its environment, and timing of the firm's strategic moves relative to the moves of other competitors in its environment. Table 5 shows the characteristics of technological strategic factors.

Table 5

Technological Strategic Factors

Factors	Intensity			
Investment in R&D	Low			High
1. R&D as % of profits	|____|____|____|____|			
2. R as % of profits	|____|____|____|____|			
3. D as % of profits	|____|____|____|____|			
Competitive Position	Imitator	Follower	Innovator	
4. Research leadership	|____|____|____|____|			
5. Product leadership	|____|____|____|____|			
6. Process leadership	|____|____|____|____|			
Product Dynamics				
7. Frequency of new products	Low			High
	|____|____|____|____|			
8. Length of life cycle	Long			Short
	|____|____|____|____|			
9. Technological advance in successive products	Small			Large
	|____|____|____|____|			
Technology dynamics				
10. Length of life cycle	Long			Short
	|____|____|____|____|			
11. Frequency of new technologies	Low			High
	|____|____|____|____|			
12. Number of competing technologies	One			Many
	|____|____|____|____|			
Competitive dynamics				
13. Technological product differentiation	None			Large
	|____|____|____|____|			
14. Technology as competitive tool	Unimportant			Key
	|____|____|____|____|			
15. Competitive intensity	Low			Intense
	|____|____|____|____|			
16. Forced product obsolescence	None			Frequent
	|____|____|____|____|			
17. Technological response to government regulations	Unimportant			Key
	|____|____|____|____|			
18. Technological response to consumer Pressures	Unimportant			Key
	|____|____|____|____|			

According to Ansoff and Antoniou (2004), the technological progress derived from the competitive dynamics of technology can be incremental, where it is expected that extensions of existing technologies will prevail, or discontinuous, where inventions of new proliferating technologies are expected to emerge.

Also, as discussed in Chapter 1, general management is responsible for the firm's strategic direction, but frequently fails to manage the organization's technological innovation process in both low and high technological industries. On one hand the focus of low technology organizations is primarily in utilizing and expanding technology innovation. On the other, technology in high technology organizations is one of the critical determining factors of firms' future success.

Furthermore, in stage 1 of his treatment of the innovation process, Bright (1969) suggests than an innovation begins with either discovery or the perception of an environment or market need or opportunity. This distinction is reflected in the innovation literature in the distinction between technology push and market pull. The technology push approach implies that a new invention is "pushed" through the R&D, production and sales function onto the market without proper consideration of whether or not it satisfies a user need. In contrast, an innovation based upon market pull has been developed by the R&D function in response to an identified market need (Martin, 1994: 43). While there are instances in which one or the other may appear to predominate, the evidence of the innovations points to the conclusion that any satisfactory theory must simultaneously take into account both elements (Freeman and Soete, 2000). High R&D investment ratios are characteristic of technology-intensive industries and puts significant requirements in management (Ansoff and McDonnell, 1990: 181-182).

50

Wen and Shih (2006) discussed that successful IT planning is considered a key determinant of long competitive advantage and innovation competency. Identifying the critical ITs and allocating research resources are two important decisions in its strategic planning. Only with a good understanding of its IT position can the firm make effective resource allocation decisions and keep its leadership. Although technological demands, technological position and technological resources are generally considered for technology prioritization, political preferences, called "influence" or "authority" may sometimes be the key factor and even have an overwhelming control of the final decision. The technological position elements of the formal scoring method that prioritizes critical ITs and allocates resources accordingly are summarized as follows:

- Losing badly: no longer a factor or is not likely to have a presence in the next five years
- Weak: behind in technology or likely to fall behind in the next five years
- Competitive: roughly even with world-best but not exclusively the strongest
- Strong: in the leading position and not in danger of losing this position in the next decade
- Unique: absolutely in the leading position and no other firms have the technology

The strength of influence preference for the technology elements of their formal scoring method are summarized as follows:

- Not important
- Slightly important
- Important

51

- Very important

- Absolutely important

<u>Information Technology Responsiveness</u>

  The main characteristics of Information Technology Responsiveness of organizational capability used in this study are based on the Strategic Success Hypothesis and Table 4 presented in Chapter 2A. For measuring capability, organizational responsiveness is measured by the openness of an organization to its environment, and the way the organization handles change. Ansoff and McDonnell (1990) discussed the technological variables on general management capability.

  Table 6 shows these variables, where check marks indicate the interdependence between strategy variables and the required general management capabilities.

Table 6

Impact of Technology on General Management Capability

Capability Components Characteristics Of Environment	Involvement in innovation management	Expertise in management of technology	Innovative Culture	Project Mgmt	Budgeting for innovation
High R&D ratio	√	√	√	√	√
Research intensive	√	√	√		
Development intensive	√	√	√		
Short product life cycles	√		√	√	
High rate of technological change	√	√	√		
State of the art products	√	√	√		
Close coupling of R&D/marketing/ Production	√		√	√	

The literature on strategic management has dealt extensively with the concept of distinctive competencies and their role in the strategic process, particularly in relation to the generation of competitive advantage and to the competitiveness construct. The development of an innovative culture that encourages knowledge-generation projects requires a change in management style, active leadership policies, training actions and suitable management models to develop innovations (Marques et al., 2006). Dosi et al. (1992: 192) distinguish between static competencies and dynamic competencies. Static competencies represent the organizational skills for replicating previously performed tasks. Dynamic competencies, on the other hand, are understood as the organization's skill in integrating, building, adapting and reconfiguring its endowment of resources so as to respond swiftly to changes in the environment, skills that are aimed explicitly at learning and the development of new products and processes.

Innovation competencies are compounded by two dimensions: Schumpeterian competencies and continuous improvement competencies (Chandy and Tellis, 1998; Damanpour, 1996; Gopalakrishnan and Damanpour, 1997). Schumpeterian competencies are based on the radical growth of knowledge stock and generative learning. They lead to discontinuous changes in the activities developed in an organization by developing new technological or organizational abilities. Continuous improvement competencies are based on the incremental growth of knowledge stock. These competencies lead to marginal changes with regard to the practices developed in the organization, strengthen the competencies and capabilities of the same. Some of the Schumpeterian distinctive competencies measurement scales considered by Marques et al. (2006) can be summarized as follows:

- Knowledge management (capability for developing knowledge management programs guaranteeing their capacity for generating knowledge and technology or for absorbing then from other organizations)

- Evaluation of knowledge (awareness by the firm of its competencies in innovation, especially with respect to key technologies, and capability for getting rid of obsolete knowledge, stimulating in exchange the search for alternative innovations)

54

- Technological proactiveness (ability to innovate to gain competitiveness by broadening the portfolio of products and technologies, rather than responding to the requirements of demand or to competitive pressure)

- Transmission of knowledge based on IT (capability of the company for using IT in order to improve information flow, develop the effective sharing of knowledge and foster communication between members of the firm)

- Technological vigilance (capability for obtaining information on the situation and progress in relevant science and technology through systems of technological vigilance)

- Incremental product and process innovation (capability for developing incremental change in products and processes)

- Radical product and process innovation (capability for developing new products and processes)

- Technological knowledge in patents (value of technological knowledge put into product and process patents)

- Depth of knowledge (organization's degree of experience in the technological and business fields prioritized in the firm strategy that enables it to keep itself at the technological leading edge in the business).

Some of the continuous improvement distinctive competencies measurement scales considered by Marques et al. (2006) can be summarized as follows:

- Rejection of tradition and encouragement of change (management commitment and ability to inspire acceptance of change in the firm, eliminating resistance to new ideas and the "sacred" nature of the dominant view)

- Focus on opportunities in assigning resources (management preference for assigning resources focused on the exploitation and/or creation of opportunities as opposed to a preference for tradition)

- Stimulating continuous improvement and change (degree in which the organization considers change as something natural and desirable, stimulating its employees to continuously question the way things are done so it can be improved, to solve problems and to offer suggestions)

- Openness to innovation (degree to which the firm supports the training and development of its employees so that they incorporate new skills, especially those required for the success of the company)

- Technological training (effectiveness in development of suitable training programs so that the firm's base of technological knowledge enables it to communicate with organizations for the dissemination of innovation and technological transfer)

- Flexibility of organizational design (degree of establishment of flexible forms of organization).

King (2006) discussed that companies that state that their objective is globalization proceed to enact that strategy. In doing so, they develop global IT capabilities to support the extensive resource exchanges that are required by globalization. Project completion largely depends on the knowledge transfer mechanisms that facilitate the importation and synthesis of information and know-how to reduce the execution and performance risk affecting Enterprise Application Integration (EAI) design and delivery. EAI projects are generally large-scale, enterprise-wide IT initiatives connecting business processes across multiple facilities and IT platforms. Using internal and external knowledge transfer mechanisms, the acquisition and integration of this knowledge is embodied in management's integrative capability (Mitchell, 2006).

Yeung et al. (1999) state that organizations that encourage learning and commitment to innovation obtain more efficient programs focused on the internal development of technological competencies. However, firms with a low degree of innovation or with high costs to develop new products will not create suitable knowledge stock to compete with other firms (Sullivan, 2001).

IT capabilities to a very large degree determine the current and future performance of modern enterprises. However, because these IT competencies and abilities depend considerably on the organization's IT architecture, this architecture has become a strategic asset for the whole organization. Yet this architecture can be either empowering and enabling or prohibitive and restrictive, determined by particular and contingent IT architectural choices (Strnadl, 2006).

In addition, top management support is the most commonly success factor when implementing complex IT projects, followed by capable and well-understood business processes, the use of a cross-functional cooperation and communication. Other significant factors are clear project goals and the management of affected employees, including training (Biehl, 2007).

Firms must combine their technology and global reach with in-depth understanding of local knowledge. The combination of local and global knowledge requires the development of native capability, an emerging business strategy built on the fact that business expansion has not only to take the needs of communities into account but also the local context, in that it has to go beyond mere integration of the local context and create synergy with it (Hart and London, 2005). Zahra et al. (2000) discussed that the conversion of knowledge into value-creating processes depends on the firm's knowledge integration mechanisms. This permits a critical, unbiased assessment of the firm's product innovation competencies and enables the cross-fertilization of ideas that ensure better decisions about refining existing competencies and developing new ones.

The capability-rigidity paradox considers how to exploit existing product innovation competencies (competence exploitation) while avoiding their dysfunctional rigidity effects by renewing and replacing them with entirely new competencies (competence exploration). In their study, Zahra et al. (2000) considered to what extent a firm has:

- Upgraded current knowledge and skills for familiar products and technologies
- Invested in enhancing skills in exploiting mature technologies that improve the productivity of current innovation operations
- Enhanced competencies in searching for solutions to customer problems that are near to existing solutions rather than completely new solutions
- Upgraded skills in product development processes in which the firm already possesses significant experience
- Strengthened knowledge and skills for projects that improve efficiency of existing innovation activities

58

- Acquired manufacturing technologies and skills entirely new to the firm

- Learned product development skills and processes (such as product design, prototyping new products, timing of new product introductions, and customizing products for local markets) entirely new to the industry

- Acquired entirely new managerial and organizational skills that are important for innovation (such as forecasting technological and customer trends; identifying emerging markets and technologies; coordinating and integrating R&D; marketing, manufacturing, and other functions; managing the product development process.

As discussed in Chapter 2A, four dimensions developed by Hofstede (1990) are used to categorize cultural differences between countries: Power distance, uncertainty avoidance, individualism-collectivism, and masculinity-femininity. Abu-Rahma (1999) used uncertainty avoidance among other managerial variables to measure the national cultural-strategic profile of Jordanian and American managers with respect to their inherent impact on strategic thinking and behavior. Uncertainty avoidance was measured by four variables. The first variable, decisions under uncertain environments, was borrowed from an instrument used by empirical studies utilizing Ansoff's strategic success formula. The other three were adopted from Hofstede (1980) and relate to:

- Rule orientation

- Employment stability

- Stress

Practical experience shows that significant changes in a firm's strategic orientation, whether introduced through formal strategic planning or as an informal process, encounter organizational resistance. The level of resistance is reduced by the extent of positive/negative loyalty which groups and individuals exhibit toward the organization and proportional to the perceived contribution to the survival/success of the organization (Ansoff and McDonnell, 1990).

Recent research provides evidence that allowing employees to participate in making decisions related to a change initiative has a positive impact on the overall success of the change (Lines, 2004). In regard to technology, it has been observed that user involvement and participation in technology decisions is of paramount importance in the successful adoption of new technology (Mirvis et al., 1991).

Schraeder et al. (2006) discussed that employees with different levels of involvement in planning technology changes will react according to attitude variables such as:

- Intent to turnover
- Job satisfaction
- Organization commitment
- Job stress

Information Technology Convergence

Knowledge Management (KM) is intrinsically a multidisciplinary concept drawing on organizational learning, organizational behavior, organizational strategy, sociology, and so on (Argote et al., 2003). A Knowledge Management System (KMS) includes the IT component of the KM initiatives and some key organizational factors that complement the technology. Advanced technologies (e.g., secure intranets, browsers with dashboards and portals, intelligent search techniques, semantic modeling of knowledge ontologies, contextual taxonomies) may be successfully deployed in KMS to manage intra- and interfirm knowledge (Kulkarni et al., 2006).

Technological convergence is the process by which industries which were once different in terms of their technological and therefore knowledge bases, come to share similar technological and knowledge bases (Rosenberg, 1976). Rosenberg used this concept to describe the process by which similar technological principles guided such diverse industrial activities as sewing machine manufacture, bicycle manufacture and firearms manufacture. In recent years examples of technological convergence, such as that between computers and communications, have actually come about by an underlying fusion of technologies, so that what appears as industries sharing similar technological principles is actually an example of technological fusion in the production of commodities (Sahal, 1985).

For a firm wishing to sell knowledge-embodied goods, technological convergence effectively enlarges the potential number of exchange transactions to encompass not one but two or more industries. It also reduces the costs of adaptation compared to the case when convergence was absent. From the point of view of the buying firm technological convergence can often make for technological complexity and the need for diversified competencies (Patel and Pavitt, 1994; Von Tunzelmann, 1996).

This may also impose severe learning, investment and supervision costs for such firms and thus make outsourcing of some technological tasks an attractive alternative. Exchange of generic knowledge in the form of bought inputs from another firm may cut down on some (though not all) of the costs of acquiring this knowledge. The situation thus becomes ripe for the emergence of a market exchange in technological knowledge-embodied goods (Athreye, 1998).

Technological convergence facilitates and reduces distance at three levels: physical distance, psycho-social distance and cultural distance. Physical distance can be reduced through communication and exchange of information using voice media such as fixed or mobile telephones, while other types require the capabilities of the Internet. Informational benefits reduce the psycho-social distance as it changes the relationship between information provider and information receiver, because they are put on an equal platform. This in turn is likely to bring changes in the value system, thereby bridging the cultural distance between different groups of people (Anand and Parashar, 2006).

To take advantage of digital convergence, industries, firms, and technology have to adjust and propose creative combinations of old and new technologies, old and new channels of distribution, and old and new corporate capabilities. The tyranny of the installed base can generate excessive inertia and resistance to change, even when better solutions are available. Firms that build scale (e.g., create large numbers in the installed base) and expand their scope (e.g., bundle technologies and services into adjacent horizontal layers) can build more enduring competitive advantage for future generations. Furthermore, competition in the new digital industries will revolve around networks and communications. If there are multiple standards, there will be less ability to communicate and interact (Yoffie, 1997).

According to MacLaghant (1998), Markus (2000), and Seeley (2000), systems integration can be defined as the unification of a company's information systems and databases to improve the process flow and focus on customer services. According to Schmidt (2000), integration can be attained at four different maturity levels. The system integration levels discussed in this study are as follows:

- Point-to-Point Integration: this level involves establishing a basic infrastructure for exchanging information between applications, although without any real business intelligence being linked to the infrastructure.

- Structural Integration: at this level companies use more advanced middleware tools to standardize and control the information exchange between applications.

- Process Integration: at this level organizations have made the transition from sharing information between applications to managing the information flow between applications.

- External Integration: at this level companies achieve external integration by real-time business applications, the transformation of business processes, and new customer-focused structures for redefining the organization.

- Unpredictable Integration: at this level the future is somewhat unpredictable as to the new tools that will be used for system integration, because innovative technologies are constantly appearing (Mendoza et al., 2006).

According to a U.S. Fixed-Mobile Convergence (FMC) survey by Dyer and Kotlyar (2007), FMC is an emerging technology with useful value-added services, but it struggles to become a priority among IT decision-makers; the market is very aware of FMC, and most firms are weighing their options; and many U.S. large business believe in FMC's benefits, but are skeptical of its ROI. To identify the level of FMC awareness in their survey, these elements were used:

- Aware of technology and considering adopting
- Aware of technology and not interested in adopting
- Not aware/never heard of technology
- Have tested this technology or submitted it to trials
- Have deployed this technology

The three most important of these features that would entice investment in FMC were used to find out the value proposition:

- Integrating employee mobile devices with the corporate telephony system
- Flat rate and reduced rate mobile calling on campus/office (in building)
- Providing integrated wired and wireless support
- Flat rate and reduced rate international mobile calling and roaming
- Removing and replacing on-premises PBX and desk phones with mobile devices that have PBX functionality
- Providing a shared office and mobile voice calling plan
- Mobile call logging/tracking using the PBX.

The following statements were used to describe survey respondents' opinion of Fixed-Mobile Convergence:

- Nice to have but not a critical application on the IT/networking roadmap
- Important to improving workforce productivity
- An important means to reduce monthly mobile communications costs
- Too expensive to deploy
- Do not understand it well enough to assess technology viability
- Over-hyped solution with few measurable results

To find out the top three barriers to deploying an FMC solution, the following factors were considered:

- Cost of solution
- Network security
- Comfortable with current telephony solutions
- Complexity of integration with existing applications or IT infrastructure
- Device limitations
- Enterprise infrastructure limitations
- Unsure of who offers this solution
- Lack of experienced vendors
- Unproven technology
- Not provided by service provider of choice

Performance on Information Technology Convergence Issues

Despite the enormous investment directed to advanced information technologies during recent years, demonstrating the effects of such investment on organizational performance has proven to be extremely complex. Over the years, several research studies have responded to this challenge by investigating the impact of IT on financial performance (Alpar and Kim, 1990; Barua et al., 1995; Bharadwaj et al., 1999); by adopting diverse conceptual, theoretical, analytical approaches; and by employing various methodologies at multiple level of analysis. But empirical studies that have examined IT payoffs have generally reported conflicting and inconclusive findings.

Although some recent studies of relationships between IT and organizational performance have reported positive and significant effects of such investment (Alpar and Kim, 1990; Barua et al., 1995; Brynjolfsson and Hitt, 1995; Lichtenberg, 1995), empirical research on the economic impacts of IT have not revealed a consistent pattern of enhanced productivity through IT investment (Loveman, 1994; Roach, 1987). From a methodological viewpoint, characteristics of the samples used, mismeasurement of output and input, inappropriate measures of firm performance, time lags due to learning and adjustments and failure to control other industry and firm specific factors that influence firm performance have been cited as the primary reasons for the unexpected results (Ahituv and Giladi, 1993; Brynjolfsson, 1993; Brynjolfsson and Hitt, 1996; Hitt and Brynjolfsson, 1996).

However, as highlighted in the study conducted by Devaraj and Kholi (2003: 274), IT payoff literature has largely overlooked IT usage, and the effects of IT adoption and usage on organizational performance have not been examined in the usage literature. Conflicting

66

results of recent empirical research could be a result of the utilization of the amount invested in IT rather than actual adoption level as an independent variable in IT performance relationships (Ataay, 2006). In this perspective, one of the goals of this study is to bridge the IT payoff and technology usage literature by examining the relationship between firms' usage level of convergence and their Performance on Information Technology Convergence Issues.

Much of the earlier work on IT impact has used the firm as the unit of analysis (Brynjolfsson, 1993). At the same time, some researchers have argued that IT effects can be identified through intermediate-level contributions (Kauffman and Kriebel, 1988). Consequently, quite a few studies have taken a process orientation to measure IT business value (Kauffman et al., 2006). A process is a structured, measured set of activities designed to produce a specified output for a particular customer or market (Davenport, 1993). Kauffman et al. consider that the development of a business process performance analysis model for the process that is being evaluated is an important step in conducting an in-depth analysis of IT impact. Such a model assesses the overall performance of a business process in the presence of variables related to IT, human factors, managerially controllable aspects, and the business environment. In such model, for IT to affect profitability, it must improve the level of process performance first and then affect the firm's economic performance. Figure 8 depicts the mechanism that delivers and quantifies IT impact.

The main indicators for the adoption and use of IT, also called IT acceptance, are user information satisfaction and system usage. DeLone and McLean (1992) developed a framework to measure the success of the acceptance of an information system or an IT tool. To investigate factors that influence senior executives to accept innovations in IT, Pijpers and

Montfort (2006) developed a theoretical research model based on the Technology

Acceptance Model developed by Davis (1989). Their research model categorized individual

characteristics, organizational characteristics, task related characteristics, and characteristics

of the IT resource. The characteristics of the IT resource were further broken down into:

- Accessibility

- Implementation process

- User interface

- Perceived ease of use

- Attitude toward use

Whitworth et al. (2006) discussed that in 1992, Apple Computer's then-CEO John

Sculley introduced the handheld Newton, saying portability (flexibility) was the wave of the

future. Even though he was right, the Newton's small size made data entry difficult, and its

handwriting recognition was poor. The flexibility advance was neutralized by a usability

reduction, and in 1998 Apple dropped the line due to poor market performance. Later, when

Palm's Graffiti language solved the usability problem, the PDA (Personal Digital Assistant)

market revived, though today, PDAs are under threat from cell phones with better

connectivity. Whitworth et al. developed a multi-dimensional model with eight performance

goals for a Web of System Performance (WOSP). They are outlined as follows (the key

goals are in parentheses):

- Boundary manages system entry to enable useful entry (extendibility) and deny
  harmful entry (security)

- Internal structure controls and sustains the system to accommodate external change (flexibility) and internal change (reliability)

- Effector manages changes on the direct environment to maximize external effects (functionality) and minimize internal effort (usability)

- Receptor manages sensing of the environment to enable meaning exchange (connectivity) and limit meaning exchange (privacy)

Of the eight WOSP goals, four are generally success-creating (functionality, flexibility, extendibility and connectivity) and four are failure-avoiding (security, reliability, privacy and usability). This is useful, as environments can vary:

- Opportunistic. Actions can yield benefits to systems that are able to rep them

- Hazardous. Actions can harm systems that cannot handle hazards

- Dynamic. The effects—loss and gain—of risk and opportunity of action can change quickly, favoring systems that do the same.

According to Lemelin (2006), the convergence of voice, data, and video over common network facilities can lead to significant cost savings in the right environment. In addition, a properly deployed converged network reduces the amount of individual network elements that need to be managed, therefore decreasing operational overhead. The elements below summarize the key drivers of convergence implementations considered for the small, mid-sized, and enterprise business market:

- Cost savings

- Support of remote workforce

- Reduced number of network elements to manage

- Disaster recovery plan

- Support of mobile workforce

- Effective technology for addressing new locations

- Converged network implementations have matured/technology is now stable/reliable

- Call center support

- Collaboration

- Investment protection

- Industry-specific application

As previously discussed in Chapter 2A, according to Ansoff and McDonnell (1990) a common practice in business firms is to use two performance objectives: Growth performance and profit performance.

The Research Questions

Based on the information presented in the previous sub-sections, a series of research questions are presented here. They are concerned with the relationships among environmental turbulence, information technology convergence, strategic innovation management and overall firm performance of middle-level managers and corporate leaders of high tech clusters in the cross-border region (San Diego, U.S. - Baja California, Mexico).

Research Question 1: What are the differences between the technological competencies of Mexican and American managers?

70

Research Question 2: What are the differences between the technology innovation focus of Mexican and American managers?

Research Question 3: What is the relationship between Information Technology Aggressiveness Gap and Performance on Information Technology Convergence Issues?

Research Question 4: What is the relationship between Information Technology Responsiveness Gap and Performance on Information Technology Convergence Issues?

Research Question 5: What is the relationship between firms' usage level of convergence and their Performance on Information Technology Convergence Issues?

Research Question 6: What is the relationship between Information Technology Convergence Gap and Performance on Information Technology Convergence Issues?

Research Question 7: What is the relationship between Information Technology Convergence and Information Technology Aggressiveness?

Research Question 8: What is the relationship between Information Technology Convergence and Information Technology Responsiveness?

Research Question 9: What is the relationship between Information Technology Convergence and Information Technology Turbulence?

Research Question 10: What is the difference between the Information Technology Environment chosen by firms' strategies in the cross-border region?

Research Question 11: What is the relationship between uncertainty avoidance and Information Technology Responsiveness?

Research Question 12: What is the difference between individuals with high levels of involvement in planning technology changes and individuals with low levels of involvement?

71

The Research Hypotheses

The specific relationships suggested by the research model to be supported with the research and based on the research questions are described as follows:

Hypothesis 1: The differences between the technological competencies of Mexican and American managers are:

1a. Mexican managers will score lower on Schumpeterian competencies than American managers.

1b. Mexican managers will score higher on continuous improvement competencies than American managers.

Hypothesis 2: The differences between the technology innovation focus of Mexican and American managers are:

2a. Mexican managers will score higher in utilizing and expanding technology innovation, where it is expected that extensions of existing technologies will prevail.

2b. Mexican managers will score lower in technology innovation as one of the critical determining factors, where inventions of new proliferating technologies are expected to emerge.

Hypothesis 3: There is a positive relationship between Information Technology Aggressiveness Gap and Performance on Information Technology Convergence Issues.

Hypothesis 4: There is a positive relationship between Information Technology Responsiveness Gap and Performance on Information Technology Convergence Issues.

72

Hypothesis 5: There is a positive relationship between firms' usage level of convergence and their Performance on Information Technology Convergence Issues.

Hypothesis 6: There is a positive relationship between Information Technology Convergence Gap and Performance on Information Technology Convergence Issues.

Hypothesis 7: There is a positive relationship between Information Technology Convergence and Information Technology Aggressiveness.

Hypothesis 8: There is a positive relationship between Information Technology Convergence and Information Technology Responsiveness.

Hypothesis 9: There is a positive relationship between Information Technology Convergence and Information Technology Turbulence.

Hypothesis 10: There is no difference between the Information Technology Environment chosen by firms' strategy in the cross-border region.

Hypothesis 11: There is a direct relationship between uncertainty avoidance and Information Technology Responsiveness.

Hypothesis 12: Individuals with high levels of involvement in planning technology changes will react more positively to the changes than individuals with low levels of involvement.

Conceptual and Operational Definitions

In this section the variables indicated in the research model are conceptually and operationally defined. Variables can be classified into four categories: Independent, Dependent, Control and Intervening (Isaac and Michael, 2005: 48).

Independent Variables

There are 4 Independent Variables: (1) Information Technology Turbulence to be used in hypotheses 3 through 9; (2) Information Technology Aggressiveness to be used in hypothesis 7; (3) Information Technology Responsiveness to be used in hypothesis 8; and (4) Information Technology Convergence to be used in hypothesis 5, and also as a dependent variable in hypotheses 7 and 8.

Information Technology Turbulence

Conceptual definitions: Information Technology Turbulence reflects the speed of change and instability of the technology environment and environmental turbulence reflects rapid market and technological changes that managers perceive as hostile and stressful conditions for their firm. Information Technology Turbulence is a combined measure of the discontinuity or changeability, predictability, and frequency of the shifts of the firm's environment.

74

Operational definition: Information Technology Turbulence is measured on a 1 (low) to 5 (high) interval: (1) repetitive; (2) expanding; (3) changing; (4) discontinuous; and (5) surprising. The level of Information Technology Turbulence is determined by the arithmetic mean of the answers from each individual respondent to the following four questions:

A. Which one of the following best describes the range of your organization's business interests?

1. Local only.

2. Domestic.

3. Cross-border (Mexico and USA).

4. Regional (such as Pacific Rim, NAFTA, ASEAN, or EU).

5. Global.

B. Which one of the following best describes the successive challenges which your firm encounters in the Technological environment?

1. Challenges are almost non-existent, dealing only with familiar challenges.

2. Challenges are slow and extrapolable from the past.

3. Challenges are fast and extrapolable from the past.

4. Challenges are new but predictable based on past experiences.

5. Challenges are new and unpredictable due to their novelty.

C. Which one of the following best describes the pace of technological changes in your industry?

1. Changes were generally much slower than my firm's ability to respond

2. Changes were somewhat slower than my firm's ability to respond

3. Changes were comparable to my firm's ability to respond

4. Changes were generally faster than my firm's ability to respond

5. Changes were usually much faster than my firm's ability to respond

D. Which one of the following best describes the predictability of technological developments in your industry?

1. Developments are much slower and totally predictable.

2. Developments are somewhat slower and forecastable.

3. Developments are rapid but predictable.

4. Developments are generally faster and partially predictable.

5. Developments are usually much faster and totally unpredictable.

Information Technology Aggressiveness

Conceptual definition: Information Technology Aggressiveness is the firm's application of strategic technological tools, techniques, and know-how to position itself in the environment and shift executive thinking about technology convergence relative to the moves of other competitors in its technological environment.

Operational definition: Information Technology Aggressiveness is measured on a 1 (low) to 5 (high) interval: (1) stable; (2) reactive; (3) anticipatory; (4) entrepreneurial; and (5) creative. The level of Information Technology Aggressiveness is determined by the arithmetic mean of the answers from each individual respondent to the following four questions:

A. To what extent does general management primarily focus on utilizing and expanding technology innovation, where it is expected that extensions of existing

76

technologies will prevail? A score of 1 means *not at all*, 2 means *slightly*, 3 means *moderately*, 4 means *very much*, 5 means *extremely*, and N/A means *not applicable*.

B. To what extent does general management primarily focus on technology innovation as one of the critical determining factors, where inventions of new proliferating technologies are expected to emerge? A score of 1 means *not at all*, 2 means *slightly*, 3 means *moderately*, 4 means *very much*, 5 means *extremely*, and N/A means *not applicable*.

C. Which one of the following best describes your company position technologically in your industry?

    1. No longer a factor or is not likely to have a presence in the next five years

    2. Behind in technology or likely to fall behind in the next five years

    3. Roughly even with world-best but not exclusively the strongest

    4. In the leading positions and is not in danger of losing this position

    5. Absolutely in the leading position and no other firms have the technology

D. Which one of the following best describes the strength of your influence preference for the technology chosen in your company? A score of 1 means *Not Important*, 2 means *Slightly Important*, 3 means *Important*, 4 means *Very Important*, and 5 means *Absolutely Important*.

Information Technology Responsiveness

Conceptual definition: Information Technology Responsiveness is defined as the propensity and ability of general management to engage in behavior that will optimize attainment of firm's long-term objectives through Schumpeterian, continuous improvement, exploitation and exploration competencies, uncertainty avoidance culture and technology changes.

Operational definition: Information Technology Responsiveness is measured on a 1 (low) to 5 (high) scale. Information Technology Responsiveness is determined by the arithmetic mean of the answers from each individual respondent to the following eighteen questions divided into five parts: (1) Six questions related to Schumpeterian Competencies; (2) five questions related to continuous improvement competencies; (3) one question related to exploitation and exploration competencies; (4) three questions related to uncertainty avoidance culture; and (5) three questions related to technology change.

Related to Schumpeterian Competencies

A. To what degree is your company aware of its competencies in innovation, especially with respect to key technologies, and capability for getting rid of obsolete knowledge, stimulating in exchange the search for alternative innovations?

78

B. To what extent is your company able to innovate and gain competitiveness by broadening the portfolio of products and technologies, rather than responding to the requirements of demand or to competitive pressure?

C. To what extent is your company capable of using IT in order to improve information flow, develop the effective sharing of knowledge and foster communication between members of the firm?

D. To what degree is your company capable of obtaining information on the situation and progress in relevant science and technology through systems of technological vigilance?

E. To what degree is your company capable of developing incremental change in products and processes?

F. To what degree is your company capable of developing new products and processes?

Related to Continuous Improvement Competencies

A. To what degree does your management have the commitment and ability to inspire acceptance of change in the firm, eliminating resistance to new ideas and the "sacred" nature of the dominant view?

B. To what extent does your management have preference for assigning resources focused on the exploitation and/or creation of opportunities as opposed to a preference for tradition?

C. To what degree does your organization consider change as something natural and desirable, stimulating its employees continuously question the way things are done so it can be improved, to solve problems and to offer suggestions?

D. To what degree does your firm support the training and development of its employees so that they incorporate new skills, especially those required for the success of the company?

E. To what extent does management develop effective suitable training programs so that the firm's base of technological knowledge enables it to communicate with organizations for the dissemination of innovation and technological transfer?

Related to Exploitation and Exploration Competencies

A. What product innovation factors does your firm consider to ensure better decisions about refining existing competencies and developing new ones? A score of 1 means *not at all*, 2 means *slightly*, 3 means *moderately*, 4 means *very much*, 5 means *extremely*, and N/A means *not applicable*.

- Upgraded current knowledge and skills for familiar products and technologies
- Invested in enhancing skills in exploiting mature technologies that improve productivity of current innovation operations
- Enhanced competencies in searching for solutions to customer problems that are near to existing solutions rather than completely new solutions
- Upgraded skills in product development processes in which the firm already possesses significant experience

- Strengthened knowledge and skills for projects that improve efficiency of existing innovation activities

- Acquired manufacturing technologies and skills entirely new to the firm

- Learned product development skills and processes (such as product design, prototyping new products, timing of new product introductions, and customizing products for local markets) entirely new to the industry

- Acquired entirely new managerial and organizational skills that are important for innovation.

Related to Uncertainty Avoidance Culture

A. Company rules should not be broken—even if the employee thinks it is in the company's best interest. A score of 1 means *Strongly disagree*, 2 means *Disagree*, 3 means *Neutral*, 4 means *Agree*, and 5 means *Strongly Agree*.

B. How long do you think you will continue to work for this company?

1. Two years at the most

2. From two to five years

3. More than five years

4. More than five years but I probably will leave before I retire

5. Until I retire

C. How often do you feel nervous or tense at work (job stress)?

Related to Technology Changes

A. What is your level of involvement in planning the technology changes in your company? A code of "1" is assigned to individuals with high levels of involvement and "2" is assigned to individuals with lower levels of involvement.

B. What is your attitude to the technology changes in your company?

C. Do you have job satisfaction after technology changes are implemented?

D. How often do you feel nervous or tense at work (job stress)?

In B, C, and D, a score of 1 means *Strongly disagree*, 2 means *Disagree*, 3 means *Neutral*, 4 means *Agree*, and 5 means *Strongly Agree*.

Information Technology Convergence

Conceptual definition: Information Technology Convergence is the degree of integration of voice, data, and video over common network facilities within the firm and their communication features ability to affect people's experience and their environment.

Operational definition: Information Technology Convergence is measured on an ordinal scale from 1 (low) to 5 (high). Information Technology Convergence is determined by the arithmetic mean of the answers from each individual respondent to the following five questions:

A. Which one of the following integration levels is your company using to improve process flow and focus on customer services?

82

1. Establishing a basic infrastructure for exchanging information between applications, although without any real business intelligence being linked to the infrastructure.

2. Using more advanced middleware tools to standardize and control the information exchange between applications.

3. Making the transition from sharing information between applications to managing the information flow between applications

4. Achieving external integration by real-time business applications, the transformation of business processes, and new customer-focused structures for redefining the organization.

5. New tools that will be used for system integration, because innovative technologies are constantly appearing.

B. Which <u>one</u> of the following best describes your level of FMC (Fixed-Mobile Convergence) awareness?

1. Not aware/never heard of technology

2. Aware of technology and not interested in adopting

3. Aware of technology and considering adopting

4. Have tested this technology or submitted it to trials

5. Have deployed this technology

C. Which <u>one</u> of the following is the most important feature that would entice you to invest in FMC (Fixed-Mobile Convergence)? A score of 1 means *not at all*, 2 means *slightly*, 3 means *moderately*, 4 means *very much*, 5 means *extremely*, and N/A means *not applicable*.

- Integrating employee mobile devices with the corporate telephony system

- Flat rate and reduced rate mobile calling on campus/office (in building)

- Providing integrated wired and wireless support

- Flat rate and reduced rate international mobile calling and roaming

- Removing and replacing on-premises PBX and desk phones with mobile devices that have PBX functionality

- Providing a shared office and mobile voice calling plan

- Mobile call logging/tracking using the PBX.

D. Which <u>one</u> of the following statements best describes your opinion of FMC (Fixed-Mobile Convergence)? A score of 1 means *not at all*, 2 means *slightly*, 3 means *moderately*, 4 means *very much*, 5 means *extremely*, and N/A means *not applicable*.

- Nice to have but not a critical application on the IT/Networking roadmap

- Important to improving workforce productivity

- An important means to reduce monthly mobile communications costs

- Too expensive to deploy

- Do not understand it to assess technology viability

- Over-hyped solution with few measurable results

E. Which <u>one</u> of the following statements best describes the top barrier to deploying an FMC (Fixed-Mobile Convergence) solution?

- Cost of solution

- Network security

- Comfortable with current telephony solutions

- Complexity of integration with existing applications or IT infrastructure

- Device limitations

- Enterprise infrastructure limitations

- Unsure of who offers this solution

- Lack of experienced vendors

- Unproven technology

- Not provided by service provider of choice

Intervening Variables

Intervening variables cannot be directly observed or measured and are hypothetical conceptions intended to explain processes between the stimulus and response. The intervening variables calculated as "gaps" are differences between Information Technology Turbulence and Information Technology Aggressiveness, Information Technology Responsiveness and Information Technology Convergence. The three intervening variables are:

Information Technology Aggressiveness Gap

Conceptual definition: Information Technology Aggressiveness Gap is the degree of misalignment between the Information Technology Aggressiveness of the firm and the Information Technology Turbulence.

Operational definition: Information Technology Aggressiveness Gap is measured by the absolute difference between the scores of the Information Technology Aggressiveness and the Information Technology Turbulence for each respondent. The range of possible scores is from 0 to 4.

Information Technology Responsiveness Gap

Conceptual definition: Information Technology Responsiveness Gap is the degree of misalignment between the Information Technology Responsiveness of the firm and the Information Technology Turbulence.

Operational definition: Information Technology Responsiveness Gap is measured by the absolute difference between the scores of the Information Technology Responsiveness and the Information Technology Turbulence for each respondent. The range of possible scores is from 0 to 4.

Information Technology Convergence Gap

Conceptual definition: Information Technology Convergence Gap is the degree of misalignment between the Information Technology Convergence of the firm and the Information Technology Turbulence.

Operational definition: Information Technology Convergence Gap is measured by the absolute difference between the scores of the Information Technology Convergence and the Information Technology Turbulence of each respondent. The range of possible scores is from 0 to 4.

Dependent Variables

There are two variables dependent on the independent variables described above, where the outcome presumably depends on how these input variables are managed or manipulated: (1) Performance on Information Technology Convergence Issues to be used in hypotheses 3 through 6; and (2) Information Technology Convergence to be used in hypotheses 7 and 8, and also as an independent variable in hypothesis 5.

Performance on Information Technology Convergence Issues

Conceptual definition: While Performance on Information Technology Convergence Issues success needs many causes, failure may need only one. It assesses firms' usage level of convergence and their Performance on Information Technology Convergence Issues, including benefits, factors and goals.

Operational definition: Performance on Information Technology Convergence Issues is determined by the arithmetic mean of the answers from each individual respondent to the following six questions using a 5-point numerical scale:

A. How valuable are these benefits of network convergence to your business? A score of 1 means *not at all*, 2 means *slightly*, 3 means *moderately*, 4 means *very much*, 5 means *extremely*, and N/A means *not applicable*.

- Cost savings

- Support of remote workforce

- Reduce number of network elements to manage

- Support of mobile workforce

- Effective technology that connects to the corporate network

- Better customer service

- Better collaboration with customers, suppliers and partners

B. What factors do you consider to accept IT convergence innovations? A score of 1 means *not at all*, 2 means *slightly*, 3 means *moderately*, 4 means *very much*, 5 means *extremely*, and N/A means *not applicable*.

- Accessibility

- Implementation process

- User interface

- Perceived ease of use

- Attitude toward use

C. What goals do you consider to evaluate IT convergence systems? A score of 1 means *not at all*, 2 means *slightly*, 3 means *moderately*, 4 means *very much*, 5 means *extremely*, and N/A means *not applicable*.

- Extendibility: Use outside component/data add-ins?

- Security: Resist outside attack/take-over?

- Flexibility: Predict/adapt to external changes?

- Reliability: Avoid/recover from internal failure?

- Functionality: What task functionality is required?

- Usability: Conserve system/user effort or training?

- Connectivity: Communicate/connect with other systems?

- Privacy: Manage self-disclosure and privacy?

D. How would you rate your overall firm performance in terms of Information Technology Convergence? A score of 1 means *poor,* 2 means *below average,* 3 means *average,* 4 means *good,* and 5 means *excellent.*

E. How would you rate your overall firm performance in terms of growth goals achieved? A score of 1 means *poor,* 2 means *below average,* 3 means *average,* 4 means *good,* and 5 means *excellent.*

F. How would you rate your overall firm performance in terms of profit goals achieved? A score of 1 means *poor,* 2 means *below average,* 3 means *average,* 4 means *good,* and 5 means *excellent.*

Summary

Chapter 2B presented the research model and the literature relevant to support the section of the global model to be studied. It described the research questions, hypotheses, and variable names, conceptual definitions and operational definitions.

The research model follows Ansoff's strategic Success Hypothesis in terms of strategic dimensions of Information Technology. The research variables were identified as Information Technology Turbulence, Information Technology Aggressiveness, Information Technology Responsiveness, Information Technology Convergence and Performance on Information Technology Convergence Issues.

Information Technology Aggressiveness drew on technological success factors, including technological progress, technological innovation process in both low and high technological industries, prioritizing critical ITs and the strength of Influence preference for the Technology. Information Technology Responsiveness assessed firm's long-term objectives through Schumpeterian, continuous improvement, exploitation and exploration competencies, uncertainty avoidance culture and technology changes.

The actual hypotheses results are detailed in Chapter 4 and their implications and conclusions will be discussed in Chapter 5.

Chapter 3

RESEARCH METHODOLOGY

This chapter describes the research methodology used in conducting the evaluation of

the proposed hypotheses in this study. The chapter includes the research strategy, research

population, sampling methodology, instrumentation, research sample, method for

establishing validity, reliability test results, data analysis methodology, and a chapter

summary.

Research Strategy

This is a strategic management research study of the relationships among the

Information Technology Environment, Information Technology Aggressiveness, Information

Technology Responsiveness, Information Technology Convergence and Performance on

Information Technology Convergence Issues. The objective of this study was to examine

certain characteristics of middle-level managers and corporate leaders of high tech clusters in

the cross-border region (San Diego, U.S. - Baja California, Mexico).

The framework developed in this study is an extension of Ansoff's Strategic Success Hypothesis. The Strategic Success Hypothesis has been empirically tested in different settings, including a cross-section of U.S. firms (Hatziantoniou, 1986); banks in the United Arab Emirates (Salameh, 1987); public serving organizations in the U.S. (Sullivan, 1987); parastatal firms in Algeria (Chabane, 1987); banks in San Diego County (Lewis, 1989); and major U.S. banks (Jaja, 1990). In all six settings, the hypothesis was statistically sustained at 0.05 or better confidence level.

The Strategic Success Hypothesis extension in this study was operationalized through four independent variables, three intervening variables, and one dependent variable. The independent variables were identified as Information Technology Turbulence, Information Technology Aggressiveness, Information Technology Responsiveness and Information Technology Convergence. The intervening variables were identified as Information Technology Aggressiveness Gap, Information Technology Responsiveness Gap and Information Technology Convergence Gap. The only dependent variable was identified as Performance on Information Technology Convergence Issues.

The descriptive-correlational design was selected to determine the relationship among the vast array of variables. Generally, the descriptive-correlational studies ask three questions: (1) What is the direction of the relationship (positive or negative)? (2) How strong is the relationship? and (3) What is the nature of the relationship? (Polkinghorne, 1983).

Research Population

The data sources were business organizations with an installed base of computer and communication technology (IT high tech clusters with middle-level managers and corporate leaders) in the cross-border region (San Diego, U.S. - Baja California, Mexico). For consistency purposes in both regions, the research targeted small and medium enterprises (SME) segment in both countries: small enterprises in the 50 to 99 employee range, and mid-sized enterprises with between 100 and 999 employees.

To increase the number of usable responses, the data collection followed different strategies in each country. A traditional mail-in survey (see Appendix A) was sent to middle-level managers and corporate leaders of SMEs in the U.S. identified through the Harte-Hanks CI Technology database (http://www.hartehanksmi.com/). The technology database contains name, function, address and phone for top managers and IT decision makers at over 543,000 businesses. However, only middle-level and corporate leaders of 584 SMEs in San Diego County were selected.

A survey (see Appendix B) was distributed to middle-level and corporate leaders of 224 SMEs in Mexico through colleagues of the researcher at: (1) The National Chamber of Commerce for Electronics, Telecommunications and Information Technology, CANIETI (Camara Nacional de la Industria Electronica, de Telecomunicaciones y Technologias de la Informacion, http://www.canieti.org/); (2) the nonprofit Information Technology and Software Cluster (Cluster de Tecnologias de Informacion y Software de Baja California, http://www.corporativovirtual.com/itbaja); (3) The Center for Scientific Research and

Graduate Studies of Ensenada (Centro de Investigacion Cientifica y de Educacion Superior de Ensenada, CICESE, http://www.cicese.mx/); (4) The North Border College (El Colegio de la Frontera Norte, COLEF, http://www.colef.mx); and (5) The Autonomous University of Baja California (Universidad Autonoma de Baja California, UABC, http://www.uabc.mx).

The data collection process took place during the period July 19 through November 9, 2007. Seventy survey questionnaires were received, thirty-two from San Diego County (5.4 percent response rate) and thirty-eight from Baja California (16.9 percent response rate).

Research Instrument

A survey questionnaire was sent to middle-level (business) and corporate leaders of SMEs in the cross-border region (San Diego, U.S. - Baja California, Mexico). A cover letter was included, describing the purpose of the study, documents for consent and brief instructions for returning it. The survey questionnaire was translated to Spanish by the researcher and certified by a professional translator (see Appendix C). An attempt was made to contact middle-level managers and corporate leaders either by by telephone or e-mail.

The survey questionnaire was developed to include all the independent and dependent variables. The variables measured by the research instrument are divided into 5 parts and each part is composed of a number of questions on 5-point Likert scales (1=low, 5=high) for assessing Information Technology Turbulence, Information Technology Aggressiveness, Information Technology Responsiveness, Information Technology Convergence and Performance on Information Technology Convergence Issues. The variables were measured as follows:

94

Information Technology Turbulence

The estimate of the value of Information Technology Turbulence was made by the manager responding to each of four attributes. A 5-point Likert scale (1=low, 5=high) was used to measure the levels of the attributes. The questions used for this measurement are:

Q1 = Complexity of environment

Q2 = Familiarity of events

Q3 = Rapidity of change

Q4 = Visibility of future

The level value for Information Technology Turbulence was calculated as follows for each survey questionnaire respondent: (Q1 + Q2 + Q3 + Q4) / 4. If a question was not answered, the score for this variable was based on the average of the remaining three questions. A history-driven environment is measured by Information Technology Turbulence of less than or equal to 3.5 and a discontinuous environment is measured by Information Technology Turbulence of greater than 3.5.

Information Technology Aggressiveness

The estimate of the value of Information Technology Aggressiveness was made by the manager responding to each of four attributes. A 5-point Likert scale (1=low, 5=high) was used to measure the levels of the attributes. The questions used for this measurement are:

Q5 = Strategic focus in utilizing and expanding technology innovation

Q6 = Strategic focus in technology innovation as critical determining factor

Q7 = Company strategic position technologically in the industry

Q8 = Strength of influence strategic preference for the Technology chosen

The level value for Information Technology Aggressiveness was calculated as follows for each survey questionnaire respondent: (Q5 + Q6 + Q7 + Q8) / 4. If a question was not answered, the score for this variable was based on the average of the remaining three questions.

Information Technology Responsiveness

The estimate of the value of Information Technology Responsiveness was made by the manager responding to each of five attributes. A 5-point Likert scale (1=low, 5=high) was used to measure the levels of the attributes. The questions used for this measurement are:

Q9 = Awareness of competencies in alternative innovations

Q10 = Ability to innovate and gain competitiveness

Q11 = Capability of using IT in order to improve information flow

Q12 = Capability of obtaining information through technological vigilance

Q13 = Capability of developing incremental change in products and processes

Q14 = Capability of developing new products and processes

Q15 = Commitment and ability to inspire acceptance of change

Q16 = Focus on the exploitation and/or creation of opportunities vs. tradition

Q17 = Consider change as natural and desirable for improvement

Q18 = Support training and development for the success of the company

Q19 = Develop training for innovation and technological transfer

Q20 = Product innovation factors for new and existing competencies

Q21 = Rule orientation

Q22 = Employment stability

Q23 = Job stress

Q24 = Technology change involvement

Q25 = Job satisfaction

For further analysis in Chapter 4, the level value for Information Technology Responsiveness was divided into 5 parts: Schumpeterian competencies (Q9 through Q14); continuous improvement competencies (Q15 through Q19); exploitation and exploration competencies (Q20); uncertainty avoidance culture (Q21 through Q23); technology changes (Q22 through Q25). The Information Technology Responsiveness level value was calculated as follows for each survey questionnaire respondent: [(Q9 + Q10 + Q11 + Q12 + Q13 + Q14) / 6 + (Q15 + Q16 + Q17 + Q18 + Q19) / 5 + (Q20) + (Q21 + Q22 + Q23) / 3 + (Q22 + Q23 + Q25) / 3] / 5. If a question was not answered, the score for this variable was based on the average of the remaining questions.

Information Technology Convergence

The estimate of the value of Information Technology Convergence was made by the manager responding to each of five attributes. A 5-point Likert scale (1=low, 5=high) was used to measure the levels of the attributes. The questions used for this measurement are:

Q26 = Fixed-Mobile Convergence integration levels

Q27 = Level of Fixed-Mobile Convergence awareness

Q28 = Features that would entice to invest in Fixed-Mobile Convergence

Q29 = Opinion of Fixed-Mobile Convergence

Q30 = Top barrier to deploy Fixed-Mobile Convergence

The level value for Information Technology Convergence was calculated as follows for each survey questionnaire respondent: (Q26 + Q27 + Q28 + Q29 + Q30) / 5. If a question was not answered, the score for this variable is based on the average of the remaining four questions.

Performance on Information Technology Convergence Issues

The estimate of the value of Performance on Information Technology Convergence Issues was made by the manager responding to each of six attributes. A 5-point Likert scale (1=low, 5=high) was used to measure the levels of the attributes. The questions used for this measurement are:

Q31 = Benefits of convergence

Q32 = Acceptance of IT convergence innovations

Q33 = Goals considered to evaluate IT convergence systems

Q34 = Information technology performance

Q35 = Growth performance

Q36 = Profit performance

The level value for Performance on Information Technology Convergence Issues was calculated as follows for each survey questionnaire respondent: (Q31 + Q32 + Q33 + Q34 + Q35 + Q36) / 6. If a question was not answered, the score for this variable is based on the average of the remaining five questions.

Any question in which N/A for *not applicable* was checked or for which no answer was selected, was not included in the above calculations. Therefore, no value for that question was added in the numerator of the equations above, and the value of the denominator was reduced once for each question answered N/A or not answered.

Information Technology Aggressiveness Gap

Information Technology Aggressiveness Gap was measured by the absolute difference between the scores of the Information Technology Aggressiveness and the Information Technology Turbulence for each respondent. The range of possible difference scores is from 0 to 4.

Information Technology Responsiveness Gap

Information Technology Responsiveness Gap was measured by the absolute difference between the scores of the Information Technology Responsiveness and the Information Technology Turbulence for each respondent. The range of possible difference scores is from 0 to 4.

Information Technology Convergence Gap

Information Technology Convergence Gap was measured by the absolute difference between the scores of the Information Technology Convergence and the Information Technology Turbulence of each respondent. The range of possible difference scores is from 0 to 4.

Methods for Establishing Validity and Reliability of Test Results

At the most general level, the two basic properties of measurement are reliability and validity (Schoenfeldt et al., 1976). Reliability refers to the extent to which a variable or set of variables is consistent in what it is intended to measure. If multiple measurements are taken, the reliable measures will all be consistent in their values. Reliability differs from validity in that it relates not to what should be measured, but instead to how it is measured (Hair et al., 2005). Although there is no absolute standard, a widely accepted threshold of reliability is 60 percent (Chadwick et al., 1984). Table 7 presents the statistical results of a reliability analysis of the variables using Cronbach's coefficient alpha (r).

Table 7

Cronbach's Coefficient Alpha of Variable-Question Relationships

Composite Variables	Questions	Number of items	Coefficient Alpha (r)
Information Technology Turbulence	1 – 4	4	≥ .5980
Information Technology Aggressiveness	5 – 8	4	≥ .6933
Information Technology Responsiveness	9 – 25	17	≥ .6788
Information Technology Convergence	26 – 30	5	≥ .8757
Performance on Information Technology Convergence issues	31 – 36	6	≥ .7876

Cronbach (1960) generalized the procedure called Kuder-Richardson formula 20

(KR-20) to the case in which differential weights or scores might be assigned to the

alternatives of several test items or to parts of a measuring instrument. A typical example in

which the coefficient alpha would be appropriate is that of estimating the internal-

consistency reliability of an attitude scale in a Likert-like format.

Pilot testing too was conducted to support the reliability. Pilot testing determines if

there are weaknesses in the design, order, or structure of the questionnaire (Emory and

Cooper, 1991). The survey questionnaire was pilot tested through researcher's acquaintances

at various high tech organizations in Southern California, including AT&T, Qualcomm,

Kyocera, and others, and two research centers in Baja California, the Center for Scientific

Research and Graduate Studies of Ensenada (Centro de Investigacion Cientifica y de

Educacion Superior de Ensenada, CICESE, http://www.cicese.mx/) and The North Border

College (El Colegio de la Frontera Norte, COLEF, http://www.colef.mx).

Validity information indicates the degree to which the test is capable of achieving

certain aims. Tests are used for several types of judgment, and for each type of judgment, a

different type of investigation is required to establish validity. The three aspects of validity

may be named content-related validity, criterion-related validity, and construct validity (Isaac

and Michael, 1997). Content-related validity requires that the questionnaire items represent

the kinds of material (or content areas) they are supposed to represent. Content validity is

used to determine whether the instrument adequately measures the topic under investigation

(Emory and Cooper, 1991). This type of validity is usually expressed either by a global, non-

quantitative judgment or in terms of the adequacy of sampling of the content to be covered.

The content validity requirement was met through intensive review by three professors at

Alliant International University: dissertation chairperson Dr. Alfred O. Lewis and
dissertation committee members Dr. Rachna Kumar and Dr. Ali Abu-Rahma.

Criterion-related validity is demonstrated by comparing the test scores with one or
more external variables considered to provide a direct measure of the characteristic or
behavior in question. This study employs various published research criteria for
Informational Technology aggressiveness, Information Technology Responsiveness and
Informational Technology Convergence. To provide a direct measure of the characteristics, a
gap analysis was conducted to measure the degree of misalignment between these variables
and the Information Technology turbulence.

The term construct-related validity is evaluated by investigating what qualities a test
measures, that is, by determining the degree to which certain explanatory concepts or
constructs account for performance on the test. In this study, all variables were measured by
the sum of varied multiple questions to produce single scores: 4 questions for Information
Technology Turbulence, 4 questions for Information Technology Aggressiveness, 18
questions for Information Technology Responsiveness, 5 questions for Information
Technology Convergence, and 6 questions for Performance on Information Technology
Convergence Issues.

Data Analysis Methodology

Partial correlations were used to test the relationships among variables. Partial correlations provide a measure of correlation between two variables by removing or adjusting for the linear effects of one or more control variables. The rationale behind the partial correlation lies in the characteristics of variables of the study measurements. As the measurements have not been generally accepted and concretely established, confirmatory zero-order correlations may be affected by spurious relationships. Acknowledging this pitfall, the study utilizes the partial correlations technique (Yum, 2000).

Data analysis was accomplished using three methods: (1) the Pearson Product-Moment Correlation Coefficient r was used to examine the relationship between variables and to reveal the magnitude and direction of the relationship; (2) a zero order multiple regression was used to analyze the relative importance among the variables; and (3) a t test was used to determine a significant difference between two sample means. The statistical tests in Table 8 show each of the hypotheses, listed with the corresponding null hypotheses. The significance of the statistical tests was determined using null hypotheses. For the purpose of this study, 5 percent is used as a threshold to assess statistical significance ($p < 0.05$).

104

Table 8

Summary of Statistical Analysis

	Research Hypothesis	Null Hypothesis	Statistical Test
1a	The differences between the technological competencies of Mexican and American managers are: Mexican managers will score lower on Schumpeterian competencies than American managers.	There are no differences between the technological Schumpeterian competencies of Mexican and American managers.	t test
1b	The differences between the technological competencies of Mexican and American managers are: Mexican managers will score higher on continuous improvement competencies than the American managers.	There are no differences between the technological continuous improvement competencies of Mexican and American managers.	t test
2a	The differences between the technological innovation focus of Mexican and American managers are: Mexican managers will score higher in utilizing and expanding technology innovation.	There are no differences between the technological innovation focus of Mexican and American managers in utilizing and expanding technology innovation, where it is expected that extensions of existing technologies will prevail.	t test
2b	The differences between the technological innovation focus of Mexican and American managers are: Mexican managers will score lower in technology innovation as one of the critical determining factors.	There are no differences between the technological innovation focus of Mexican and American managers as one of the critical determining factors, where inventions of new proliferating technologies are expected to emerge.	t test
3	There is a positive relationship between Information Technology Aggressiveness Gap and Performance on Technology Convergence Issues.	There is no relationship between Information Technology Aggressiveness Gap and Performance on Information Technology Convergence Issues.	Correlation (Pearson's r)

4	There is a positive relationship between Information Technology Responsiveness Gap and Performance on Information Technology Convergence Issues.	There is no relationship between Information Technology Responsiveness Gap and Performance on Information Technology Convergence Issues.	Correlation (Pearson's r)
5	There is a positive relationship between firms' usage level of convergence and their Performance on Information Technology Convergence Issues.	There is no relationship between firms' usage level of convergence and their Performance on Information Technology Convergence Issues.	Correlation (Pearson's r)
6	There is a positive relationship between Information Technology Convergence Gap and Performance on Information Technology Convergence Issues.	There is no relationship between Information Technology Convergence Gap and Performance on Information Technology Convergence Issues.	Correlation (Pearson's r)
7	There is a positive relationship between Information Technology Convergence and Information Technology Aggressiveness.	There is no relationship between Information Technology Convergence and Information Technology Aggressiveness.	Correlation (Pearson's r)
8	There is a positive relationship between Information Technology Convergence and Information Technology Responsiveness.	There is no relationship between Information Technology Convergence and Information Technology Responsiveness.	Correlation (Pearson's r)
9	There is a positive relationship between Information Technology Convergence and Information Technology Turbulence.	There is no relationship between Information Technology Convergence and Information Technology Turbulence.	Correlation (Pearson's r)
10	There is no difference between the Information Technology Environment chosen by firms' strategy in the cross-border region.	There is a difference between the Information Technology Environment chosen by firms' strategy in the cross-border region.	t test
11	There is a direct relationship between uncertainty avoidance and Information Technology Responsiveness.	There is no relationship between uncertainty avoidance and Information Technology Responsiveness.	Correlation (Pearson's r)

12	Individuals with high levels of involvement in planning the technology changes will react more positively to the changes than individuals with low levels of involvement.	Individuals with high levels of involvement in planning the technology changes will not react more positively to the changes than individuals with low levels of involvement.	t test

Assumptions and Limitations

The respondents understood the wording of the survey questionnaire. The respondents gave honest answers to the best of their knowledge and ability. This study was limited to the research model presented in section 2B, Figure 8 that is embedded in the Global Model presented in Chapter 2A, Figure 3. The samples were selected from cross-border region organizations (San Diego, U.S. - Baja California, Mexico). Appendix D presents the values for the research variables calculated from the responses in each returned survey.

Summary

This chapter describes the research methodology used in conducting the evaluation of the 12 proposed hypotheses in this study. The research strategy is an extension of the Ansoff Strategic Success Hypothesis, which is operationalized through four independent variables, three intervening variables, and one dependent variable. The descriptive-correlational design was selected to determine the relationship among the vast array of variables. The research population was collected through the Harte-Hanks CI Technology database from middle-level (business) and corporate leaders of 584 SMEs in San Diego County, U.S., and through partnerships with local chambers of commerce, nonprofit Information Technology clusters, Research Centers and Universities from middle-level managers and corporate leaders of approximately 224 SMEs in Baja California, Mexico.

As a research instrument, a 36-question survey questionnaire was developed in English and Spanish to include all the independent and dependent variables. The variables measured by the research instrument were divided into 5 parts and each part is composed of a number of questions on 5-point Likert scales (1=low, 5=high). The method for establishing validity was using three aspects of validity, named content-related validity, criterion-related validity, and construct validity. The reliability test results analysis of the variables was provided using Cronbach's coefficient alpha (r). Pilot testing too was conducted to support the reliability.

The data analysis methodology consisted of the Pearson Product-Moment Correlation Coefficient r to examine the relationship between variables and to reveal the magnitude and direction of the relationship, a zero order multiple regression to analyze the relative importance among the variables, and a t test to determine a significant difference between two sample means.

Appendix A presents the survey questionnaire that was sent to 584 middle-level managers and corporate leaders of SMEs in the U.S. identified through the Harte-Hanks CI Technology database. Appendix B presents the survey that was distributed to middle-level and corporate leaders of 224 SMEs in Mexico through colleagues of the researcher at chambers of commerce, research centers and universities. Appendix C presents the English

108

to Spanish translation certification letter provided by a court interpreter/translator duly authorized and certified by the Superior Court of Justice of Baja California, Mexico. Appendix D presents the values for the research variables calculated from the responses in each returned survey.

The data collection process took place during the period July 19 through November 9, 2007. Seventy survey questionnaires were received, thirty-two from San Diego County (5.4 percent response rate) and thirty-eight from Baja California, Mexico (16.9 percent response rate).

Chapter 4

RESEARCH FINDINGS

This chapter presents the results of the data analysis of the study. Chapter 4 is divided into four sections: (1) descriptive statistics, (2) hypotheses test results, (3) additional statistical analysis and (4) chapter summary.

<u>Descriptive Statistics</u>

To describe the basic features of the data in this study summaries about the sample and the measures are provided. Table 9 presents the variable name, mean, and standard deviation for the data collected in this study.

Table 9

Descriptive Statistics (N = 70)

Variable Name	Mean	Standard Deviation	Range Min	-	Max
IT Turbulence	3.42	0.629	1.75	-	4.75
IT Aggressiveness	3.26	0.631	2.00	-	5.00
IT Responsiveness	3.46	0.528	2.34	-	4.44
IT Convergence	3.10	0.684	1.33	-	4.21
IT Aggressiveness Gap	0.56	0.467	0.00	-	1.75
IT Responsiveness Gap	0.58	0.475	0.00	-	1.94
IT Convergence Gap	0.71	0.559	0.04	-	2.25
Performance on IT Convergence Issues	3.56	0.502	2.39	-	5.00

Hypotheses Test Results

In this section, the findings concerning the 12 research questions and associated hypotheses are presented and analyzed.

Hypothesis 1

Hypothesis 1 was divided into two parts. Hypothesis 1a predicted that Mexican managers would score lower on Schumpeterian technological competencies than American managers. Hypothesis 1a was not supported. Hypothesis 1b predicted that Mexican managers would score higher on continuous improvement competencies than American managers. Hypothesis 1b was not supported. Table 10 shows the results of the t tests.

Table 10

Differences of Mexican and American Managers in Technological Competencies

	Test of Hypothesis	N	Means	t test	Significance, p	Hypothesis Supported ?
1a	Schumpeterian technological competencies (38 Baja California managers versus 32 San Diego County managers)	70	3.504 versus 3.694	-1.020	≤ 0.314	No
1b	Continuous improvement competencies (38 Baja California managers versus 32 San Diego County managers)	70	3.750 versus 3.820	-0.400	≤ 0.691	No

Hypothesis 2

Hypothesis 2 was divided into two parts. Hypothesis 2a predicted that Mexican managers would score higher in utilizing and expanding technology innovation, where it is expected that extensions of existing technologies will prevail. Hypothesis 2a was not supported. Hypothesis 2b predicted that Mexican managers would score lower in technology innovation as one of the critical determining factors, where inventions of new proliferating technologies are expected to emerge. Hypothesis 2b was supported in favor of Mexican managers at the 5 percent level (2-tailed) and deserves further research. Table 11 shows the results of the *t* tests.

Table 11

Differences of Mexican and American Managers - Innovation Focus

	Test of Hypothesis	N	Means	*t* test	Significance, p	Hypothesis Supported ?
2a	Utilizing and expanding technology innovation (38 Baja California managers versus 32 San Diego County managers)	70	3.316 versus 3.125	0.761	≤ 0.449	No
2b	Innovation as one of the critical determining factors (38 Baja California managers versus 32 San Diego County managers)	70	3.632 versus 2.938	2.062	≤ 0.043	Yes

113

Hypothesis 3

Hypothesis 3 predicted a positive relationship between Information Technology Aggressiveness Gap and Performance on Information Technology Convergence Issues. It was expected that Performance on Information Technology Convergence Issues would be higher when the Information Technology Aggressiveness Gap was lower. Hypothesis 3 was not supported. Figure 9 displays the data points and the resulting regression line, along with the statistics of the regression. As the gap between Information Technology Aggressiveness and Information Technology Turbulence increased, Performance on Information Technology Convergence Issues decreased. No correlation was found.

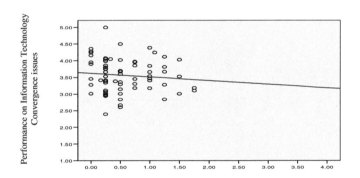

Information Technology Aggressiveness Gap

O   Data   ————   Regression
Regression slope = -0.108, regression intercept = 3.621, correlation coefficient r = -0.101, coefficient of determination r^2 = 0.010, p < 0.408, N = 70.

Figure 9
Statistical Results for Hypothesis 3

Hypothesis 4

Hypothesis 4 predicted a positive relationship between Information Technology Responsiveness Gap and Performance on Information Technology Convergence Issues. It was expected that Performance on Information Technology Convergence Issues would be higher when the Information Technology Responsiveness Gap was lower. Hypothesis 4 was not supported. Figure 10 displays the data points and the resulting regression line, along with the statistics of the regression. As the gap between Information Technology Responsiveness and Information Technology Turbulence increased, Performance on Information Technology Convergence Issues decreased.

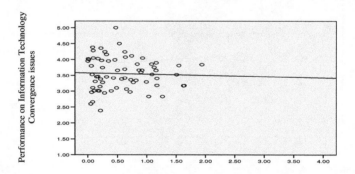

Information Technology Responsiveness Gap

○ Data ——— Regression

Regression slope = -0.039, regression intercept = 3.582, correlation coefficient r = -0.037, coefficient of determination r^2 = 0.001, $p < 0.761$, $N = 70$.

Figure 10
Statistical Results for Hypothesis 4

Hypothesis 5

Hypothesis 5 predicted a positive relationship between firms' usage level of convergence and their Performance on Information Technology issues. It was expected that Performance on Information Technology Convergence Issues would be higher when firms' usage level of convergence was higher. Hypothesis 5 was supported. Figure 11 displays the data points and the resulting regression line, along with the statistics of the regression. As the firms' usage level of convergence increased, Performance on Information Technology Convergence Issues increased. The results were significant at the 0.1 percent level (2-tailed).

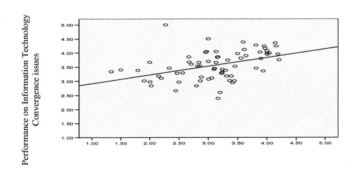

Firm's usage Level of Convergence

○ Data ——— Regression

Regression slope = 0.307, regression intercept = 2.608, correlation coefficient r = 0.419 (moderate), coefficient of determination r^2 = 0.175, $p < 0.001$, N = 70.

Figure 11
Statistical Results for Hypothesis 5

Hypothesis 6

Hypothesis 6 predicted a positive relationship between Information Technology Convergence Gap and Performance on Information Technology Convergence Issues. It was expected that Performance on Information Technology Convergence Issues would be higher when the Information Technology Convergence Gap was lower. Hypothesis 6 was not supported. Figure 12 displays the data points and the resulting regression line, along with the statistics of the regression. As the gap between Information Technology Convergence and Information Technology Turbulence increased, Performance on Information Technology Convergence Issues decreased.

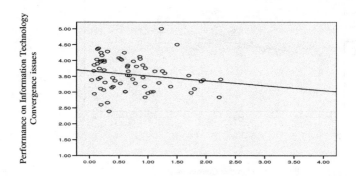

Information Technology Convergence Gap

⭘ Data ——— Regression

Regression slope = -0.154, regression intercept = 3.670, correlation coefficient r = -0.173, coefficient of determination r^2 = 0.029, $p < 0.153$, $N = 70$.

Figure 12
Statistical Results for Hypothesis 6

117

Hypothesis 7

Hypothesis 7 predicted a positive relationship between Information Technology Convergence and Information Technology Aggressiveness. It was expected that firms' usage level of convergence would be higher when Information Technology Aggressiveness was higher. Hypothesis 7 was supported. Figure 13 displays the data points and the resulting regression line, along with the statistics of the regression. As the Information Technology Aggressiveness increased, firms' usage level of convergence increased. The results were significant at the 0.5 percent level (2-tailed).

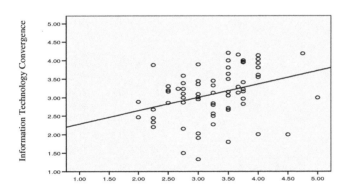

Information Technology Aggressiveness

O Data ——— Regression

Regression slope = 0.361, regression intercept = 1.921, correlation coefficient r = 0.333 (moderate), coefficient of determination r^2 = 0.110, p < 0.005, N = 70.

Figure 13
Statistical Results for Hypothesis 7

Hypothesis 8

Hypothesis 8 predicted a positive relationship between Information Technology Convergence and Information Technology Responsiveness. It was expected that firms' usage level of convergence would higher when Information Technology Responsiveness was higher). Hypothesis 8 was supported. Figure 14 displays the data points and the resulting regression line, along with the statistics of the regression. As the Information Technology Responsiveness increased, firms' usage level of convergence increased. The results were significant at the 0.1 percent level (2-tailed).

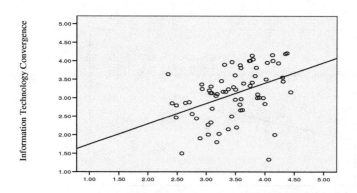

Information Technology Responsiveness

O   Data   ⸻   Regression

Regression slope = 0.551, regression intercept = 1.193, correlation coefficient r = 0.425 (moderate), coefficient of determination r^2 = 0.180, $p < 0.001$, $N = 70$.

Figure 14
Statistical Results for Hypothesis 8

Hypothesis 9

Hypothesis 9 predicted a positive relationship between Information Technology Convergence and Information Technology Turbulence. It was expected that firms' usage level of convergence would be higher when Information Technology Turbulence was higher). Hypothesis 9 was not supported. Figure 15 displays the data points and the resulting regression line, along with the statistics of the regression. As the Information Technology Turbulence increased, firms' usage level of convergence increased.

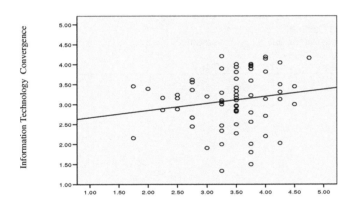

Information Technology Turbulence

O Data ——— Regression

Regression slope = 0.176, regression intercept = 2.493, correlation coefficient r = 0.163, coefficient of determination r^2 = 0.026, p < 0.179, N = 70.

Figure 15
Statistical Results for Hypothesis 9

120

Hypothesis 10

Hypothesis 10 predicted that there would be no difference between the Information

Technology Environment chosen by firms' strategy in the cross-border region. Hypothesis 10

was supported. Table 12 shows the results of the *t* test.

Table 12

Differences of Firm's Strategy in the Cross-border Region

	Test of Hypothesis	N	Means	*t* test	Significance, p	Hypothesis Supported ?
10	IT Environment chosen (38 Baja California Managers versus 32 San Diego County Managers)	70	3.388 versus 3.461	-0.500	$\leq$ 0.622	Yes

Hypothesis 11

Hypothesis 11 predicted a direct relationship between uncertainty avoidance and Information Technology Responsiveness. It was expected that uncertainty avoidance would be higher when Information Technology Responsiveness was higher. Hypothesis 11 was supported. Figure 16 displays the data points and the resulting regression line, along with the statistics of the regression. As the Information Technology Responsiveness increased, uncertainty avoidance increased. The results were significant at the 0.1 percent level (2-tailed).

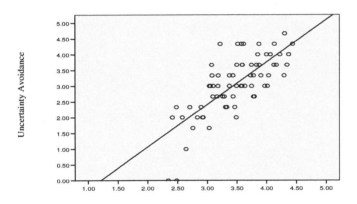

Information Technology Responsiveness

O   Data   ——————   Regression

Regression slope = 0.414, regression intercept = 2.203, correlation coefficient $r = 0.747$ (strong), coefficient of determination $r^2 = 0.557$, $p < 0.001$, $N = 70$.

Figure 16
Statistical Results for Hypothesis 11

Hypothesis 12

Hypothesis 12 predicted that individuals with high levels of involvement in planning the technology changes would react more positively to the changes than individuals with low levels of involvement. Hypothesis 12 was supported. Table 13 shows the results of the *t* test.

Table 13

Differences of Individuals in Planning the Technology Changes

	Test of Hypothesis	N	Means	*t* test	Significance, p	Hypothesis Supported ?
12	Level of involvement (29 Managers with Low Involvement versus 41 Managers with High Involvement)	70	3.552 versus 4.317	-3.20	≤ 0.003	Yes

Note: Pearson correlation coefficient r = 0.383 (moderate)

Additional Statistical Analysis

The results of the statistical analyses supported the original hypothesis that Performance on Information Technology Convergence Issues would be optimal when firms' usage level of convergence, Information Technology Aggressiveness and Information Technology Responsiveness were aligned in an organization. Therefore, a firm's Performance on Information Technology Convergence Issues would be optimal when the information technology aggressiveness of the firm's strategic behavior matched the turbulence of its technological environment, the responsiveness of the firm's technology capability matched the aggressiveness of its strategy and the components of the firm's technology capability were supportive of one another. Three additional analyses were performed to explain the Strategic Success Hypothesis where performance is expected to be optimal when there is alignment in an organization among environmental turbulence, strategic aggressiveness and responsiveness of organizational capability.

Hypothesis 13

Hypothesis 13 predicted a positive relationship between Information Technology Turbulence and their Performance on Information Technology issues. It was expected that Performance on Information Technology Convergence Issues would be higher when Information Technology Turbulence was higher. Hypothesis 13 was supported. Figure 17 displays the data points and the resulting regression line, along with the statistics of the regression. As the Information Technology Turbulence increased, Performance on Information Technology Convergence Issues increased. The results were significant marginally at the 5.3 percent level (2-tailed).

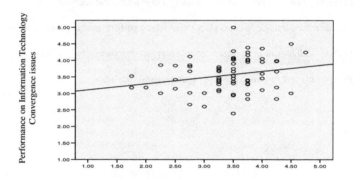

Information Technology Turbulence

O Data ——— Regression

Regression slope = 0.185, regression intercept = 2.925, correlation coefficient r = 0.233 (weak), coefficient of determination r^2 = 0.054, p < 0.053 (marginal), N = 70.

Figure 17
Statistical Results for Hypothesis 13

Hypothesis 14

Hypothesis 14 predicted a positive relationship between Information Technology

Aggressiveness and their Performance on Information Technology issues. It was expected

that Performance on Information Technology Convergence Issues would be higher when

Information Technology Aggressiveness was higher. Hypothesis 14 was supported. Figure

18 displays the data points and the resulting regression line, along with the statistics of the

regression. As the Information Technology Aggressiveness increased, Performance on

Information Technology Convergence Issues increased. The results were significant at the

0.1 percent level (2-tailed).

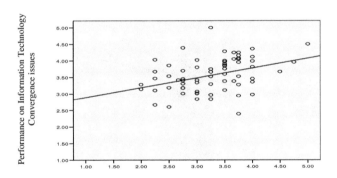

Information Technology Aggressiveness

O   Data   ———— Regression

Regression slope = 0.296, regression intercept = 2.593, correlation coefficient r = 0.373 (moderate), coefficient
of determination r^2 = 0.139, p < 0.001, N = 70.

Figure 18
Statistical Results for Hypothesis 14

Hypothesis 15

Hypothesis 15 predicted a positive relationship between Information Technology Responsiveness and their Performance on Information Technology issues. It was expected that Performance on Information Technology Convergence Issues would be higher when Information Technology Responsiveness was higher. Hypothesis 15 was supported. Figure 19 displays the data points and the resulting regression line, along with the statistics of the regression. As the Information Technology Responsiveness increased, Performance on Information Technology Convergence Issues increased. The results were significant at the 0.2 percent level (2-tailed).

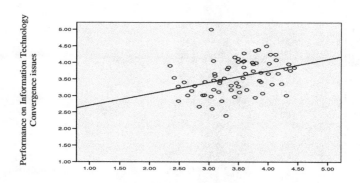

Information Technology Responsiveness

○ Data —————— Regression

Regression slope = 0.348, regression intercept = 2.354, correlation coefficient r = 0.367 (moderate), coefficient of determination r^2 = 0.134, p < 0.002, N = 70.

Figure 19
Statistical Results for Hypothesis 15

Cross-Tabulation of Variables

Table 14 presents a cross-tabulation of the linear regression coefficients and the corresponding statistical significance for the nine variables in this study. The table indicates which correlations correspond to the twelve hypotheses that were tested using linear regression.

Table 14

Cross-Tabulation of the Correlation of Research Variables

	IT Turbulence	IT Aggressiveness	IT Responsiveness	IT Convergence	IT Aggressiveness Gap	IT Responsiveness Gap	IT Convergence Gap	Uncertainty Avoidance
IT Aggressiveness	r = 0.356 p< 0.002							
IT Responsiveness		r = 0.484 p< 0.001						
IT Convergence		r = 0.333 p< 0.005 H7	r = 0.425 p< 0.001 H8					
IT Aggressiveness Gap		r =-0.308 p< 0.010						
IT Responsiveness Gap					r = 0.401 p< 0.001			
IT Convergence Gap					r =-0.620 p< 0.001	r = 0.339 p< 0.004	r = 0.421 p< 0.001	
Uncertainty Avoidance			r = 0.747 p< 0.001 H11					
Performance on IT Convergence Issues	r = 0.233 p< 0.053 H13	r = 0.373 p< 0.001 H14	r = 0.367 p< 0.002 H15	r = 0.419 p< 0.001 H5				

N = 70,   H# = Hypothesis #,   **Correlations significant at p < 0.05 are shown in bold.**
Correlations significant at p < 0.01 are shown in bold and shaded.

Summary of Results

This chapter presented the statistical results of the data analysis of this study. The results of all of the statistical analyses are summarized in Table 15. No significant differences in the technological competencies of Mexican and American managers were found in hypothesis 1. Hypothesis 1a predicted that Mexican managers would score lower on Schumpeterian technological competencies. Hypothesis 1b predicted that Mexican managers would score higher on continuous improvement competencies. Neither hypothesis was supported. Hypothesis 2 analyzed differences in the innovation focus of Mexican and American managers. Hypothesis 2a predicted that Mexican managers would score higher in utilizing and expanding technology innovation. Hypothesis 2a was not supported. Hypothesis 2b predicted that Mexican managers would score lower in technology innovation as one of the critical determining factors. Hypothesis 2b was supported, but in favor of Mexican Managers.

Hypotheses 3 and 4 expected that Performance on Information Technology Convergence Issues would higher when Information Technology Aggressiveness and Responsiveness Gaps were lower. Neither hypothesis was supported. Hypotheses 5, 7 and 8 predicted that when firms' usage level of convergence increased, Performance on Information Technology Convergence Issues, Information Technology Aggressiveness and Information Technology Responsiveness would also increase. The results of these three hypotheses were significant at the 0.5 percent level or better. However, hypothesis 6 was not supported. Hypothesis 6 predicted that as the gap between Information Technology

129

Convergence and Information Technology Turbulence increased, Performance on

Information Technology Convergence Issues would decrease. Hypothesis 9 predicted that as

the Information Technology Turbulence increased, firms' usage level of convergence would

increase. This hypothesis was not supported.

Hypothesis 10 predicted that there would be no difference between the Information

Technology Environment chosen by firms' strategy in the cross-border region. Hypothesis 10

was supported. Hypothesis 11 predicted that as Information Technology Responsiveness

increased, uncertainty avoidance would also increase. The results were significant at the 0.01

percent level. Hypothesis 12 predicted that individuals with high levels of involvement in

planning technology changes will react more positively to the changes than individuals with

low levels of involvement. Hypothesis 12 was supported.

Additional statistical analyses were performed to support the Strategic Success

Hypothesis. Hypotheses 14 and 15 predicted that Performance on Information Technology

Convergence Issues would increase as Information Technology Aggressiveness and

Responsiveness increased. The results were significant at the 0.05 percent level or better.

Hypothesis 13 was marginally supported.

Table 15

Summary of Statistical Results (N = 70)

	Research Hypothesis	r/t	p	Supported?
	Hypotheses tested by t tests			
1a	Mexican managers will score lower on Schumpeterian competencies than American managers.	-1.020	< 0.314	No
1b	Mexican managers will score higher on continuous improvement competencies than the American managers.	-0.400	< 0.691	No
2a	Mexican managers will score higher in utilizing and expanding technology innovation.	0.761	< 0.449	No
2b	Mexican managers will score lower in technology innovation as one of the critical determining factors.	2.062	< 0.043	Yes
10	There is no difference between the Information Technology Environment chosen by firms' strategy in the cross-border region.	-0.500	< 0.622	Yes
	Hypotheses tested by correlation (Pearson's r)			
3	There is a positive relationship between IT Aggressiveness Gap and Performance on Information Technology Convergence Issues.	-0.101	< 0.408	No
4	There is a positive relationship between IT Responsiveness Gap and Performance on Information Technology Convergence Issues.	-0.037	< 0.761	No
5	There is a positive relationship between firms' usage level of convergence and their Performance on Information Technology Convergence Issues.	0.419	< 0.001	Yes
6	There is a positive relationship between IT Convergence Gap and Performance on Information Technology Convergence Issues.	-0.173	< 0.153	No
7	There is a positive relationship between IT Convergence and IT Aggressiveness.	0.333	< 0.005	Yes
8	There is a positive relationship between IT Convergence and IT Responsiveness.	0.425	< 0.001	Yes
9	There is a positive relationship between IT Convergence and IT Turbulence.	0.163	< 0.179	No
11	There is a direct relationship between uncertainty avoidance and IT Responsiveness.	0.747	< 0.001	Yes
12	Individuals with high levels of involvement in planning technology changes will react more positively to the changes.	0.383	< 0.003	Yes

Additional Statistical Results. Hypotheses tested by correlation (Pearson's r)				
13	There is a positive relationship between IT Turbulence and Performance on Information Technology Convergence Issues.	0.233	< 0.053	Yes
14	There is a positive relationship between IT Aggressiveness and Performance on Information Technology Convergence Issues.	0.373	< 0.001	Yes
15	There is a positive relationship between IT Responsiveness and Performance on Information Technology Convergence Issues.	0.367	< 0.002	Yes

Chapter 5

SUMMARY, CONCLUSIONS, AND RECOMMENDATIONS

This chapter presents a summary of Chapters 1 through 4. It also presents

conclusions based on the findings, assumptions and limitations, and recommendations for

future research.

Summary of Chapters 1 through 4

Chapter 1 presented the background of the problem, the importance of information

technology convergence, the need to manage strategic innovation, a statement of the problem,

the expected contributions to the academic field of strategic management and application to

the practice of management. Chapter 2A presented the conceptual design of the global

model of all variables and relationships depicted in the model and a narrative discussion of

the flow through the model. Chapter 2B presented the conceptual design of the research

model as a section of the global model studied and included literature to support the research

questions that address the problem, the research hypotheses and variable names, and the

conceptual and operational definitions. Chapter 3 presented the research methodology used

in conducting the evaluation of the proposed hypotheses in this study, the research strategy,

research population, sampling methodology, instrumentation, research sample, method for establishing validity, reliability test results and data analysis methodology. Chapter 4 presented the results of the data analysis of the study, including descriptive statistics, hypotheses test results, and additional statistical analysis.

Background of the Problem

Schumpeter followed the Russian economist Kondratieff to describe waves of technical change as "successive industrial revolutions." Per Schumpeter, we are in the fifth Kondratieff wave since the 1990s, with a variety of technical innovations in microelectronics, computer, and research and development global networks.

The variety of innovations during the waves of technical change includes the invention of the telephone, the world's first electrical digital computer, the cellular telephone service, Information Theory, the eventual creation of integrated circuits (microprocessors) that contain millions of transistors, long-distance television transmission and the core protocols of today's Internet, TCP/IP among others.

The different innovations of the Information Technology trio commonly called "triple play" today (voice, video, and data) were originally developed in different domains, and the networks carrying them were designed and engineered specifically for their requirements. The implication was that different network environments had to be supported concurrently to allow all three services to exist.

Technological convergence is the process by which industries which were once different in terms of their technological and therefore knowledge bases, come to share similar technological and knowledge bases (Rosenberg, 1976).

134

The knowledge and information revolution began at the turn of the twentieth century and has gradually accelerated. Furthermore, significant discontinuities such as globalization, deregulation, blurring of industry boundaries through new business models, technological convergence and disintermediation pose new managerial challenges forcing managers to create new competencies. Indeed, the combination of the personal computer, the microprocessor, the Internet, and fiber optics fostered and demanded new business practices and types of skills which were less about vertical chain of command for value creation and more about connecting and collaborating horizontally for value creation.

In addition, in a business environment characterized by rapid and disruptive technological changes, incumbents have to acquire new technological capabilities and explore new business opportunities in order to stay profitable in the long run.

While the potential advantages of convergence are undisputed, they remain to be demonstrated in practice for most areas, and the promised economies and savings need to be documented (Fowler, 2005: 16). How much substance is behind the digital convergence hype? Are we on the verge of a true technological revolution that will reshape the global economy? What should companies and managers do to prepare for such a turbulent competitive environment? (Yoffie, 1997: 1).

Statement of the Problem

This strategic management research study was concerned with empirical research that relates environmental turbulence, information technology convergence, strategic innovation management and Performance on Information Technology Convergence Issues. The study hypothesized that when environmental turbulence associated with technological issues, innovative service delivery strategies implemented through strategic aggressiveness, and required responsiveness of organizational capability are aligned in an organization, performance on convergence issues is expected to be optimal.

Purpose of the Study

The focus of the study was on high tech clusters in the cross-border region (San Diego, U.S. - Baja California, Mexico), the technological-innovation differences between middle-level managers and corporate leaders, and thus performance on convergence issue differences in both countries. The study addressed organizations' technology convergence innovation process in both low and high technological industries. It also hypothesized that the focus of low technology organizations is primarily on utilizing and expanding technology convergence innovation, and that technology convergence in high technology organizations is one of the critical determining factors of firms' future success.

136

Contributions to the Academic Field of Strategic Management

The expected contributions of this study from an academic perspective were to provide empirical evidence about the relationships among environmental turbulence associated with technological issues, innovative service delivery strategies implemented through strategic aggressiveness, required responsiveness of organizational capability, and Performance on Information Technology Convergence Issues.

Contributions to the Practice of Management

The expected contributions and application to the practice of management focused on the appropriate use of technology convergence strategies in low and high technology organizations in the cross-border region (San Diego, U.S. - Baja California, Mexico) and on ways to help managers identify convergence drivers for their firms' future success.

General Theoretical Framework

The primary framework under which this study was conducted is based on Ansoff's Strategic Success Hypothesis (Ansoff and McDonnell, 1990). However, this study also focused on relevant insights from the knowledge-based theory and the resource-based view of the firm to conduct research through Knowledge Management processes, mechanisms and strategic dimensions of technology that can be used to facilitate knowledge integration across business and Information Technology such as Schumpeterian and continuous improvement

137

competencies and their role in the strategic process, and the effects of IT adoption and usage on organizational performance. The general theoretical framework is presented in the Global Model depicted in Figure 20.

Description of the Global Model

The global model shown in Figure 20 is divided into four sections. The top section, labeled (1), contains environmental and IT turbulences and the interactions with the firm. The section below, labeled (2), includes business-technology strategies, synergies and the relationships with the external environmental and IT turbulences. The section below, labeled (3), shows the strategic business, technological capabilities and their synergies through the Strategic Success Hypothesis and the importance of technology (Theorem 2.4). The bottom section, labeled (4), shows downstream coupling and interactions with business and technological areas.

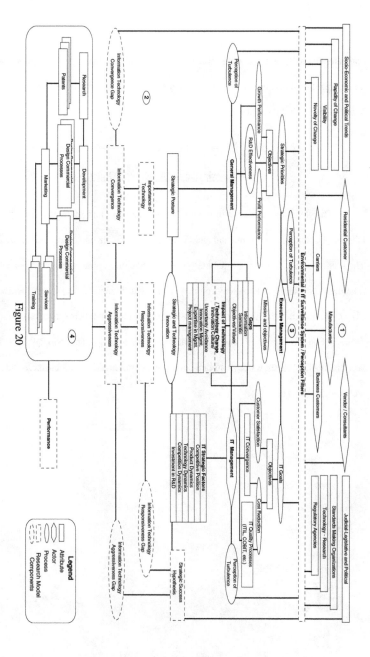

The Global Model

Figure 20

139

Synergies, Interactions and Relationships with the Firm

According to the Strategic Success Hypothesis, when environmental turbulence, strategic aggressiveness, and responsiveness of organizational capability are aligned in an organization, performance is expected to be optimal (Ansoff and McDonnell, 1990). The respective levels of turbulence are described as a combined measure of the discontinuity or changeability, predictability, and frequency of the shifts of the firm's environment. At the lowest turbulence level (1), the business environment is placid and a firm can confine its attention to its historical marketplace, successive challenges are a repetition of the past, change is slower than the firm's ability to respond and the future is expected to replicate the past. At the highest turbulence level (5), a small (but growing) and important group of industries consists of the creators of economic and technological progress. These are the high tech industries, born of novel technologies.

The concept of strategic aggressiveness is measured by two characteristics: discontinuity of a firm's consecutive strategic moves in its environment, and timing of the firm's strategic moves relative to the moves of other competitors in its environment. For measuring capability, Ansoff and McDonnell (1990) used organizational responsiveness measured by the openness of an organization to its environment, and the way the organization handles change. Table 16 shows the characteristics of strategic aggressiveness and responsiveness that match the 5-point scale of discrete turbulence environmental levels.

140

Table 16

Environmental Turbulence, Strategic Aggressiveness, and Responsiveness of Organizational Capability

Turbulence Characteristic	Turbulence Level				
	1	2	3	4	5
	Repetitive	Expanding	Changing	Discontinuous	Surprising
Turbulence					
Complexity	National	+	Regional	+	Global
Familiarity of Events	Familiar	Extrapolable		Discontinuous familiar	Discontinuous Novel
Rapidity of Change	Slower than response		Comparable to response		Faster than response
Visibility of Future	Recurring	Forecastable	Predictable	Partially predictable	Unpredictable surprises
Strategic aggressiveness	Stable, based on precedents	Reactive incremental, based on experience	Anticipatory incremental, based on extrapolation	Entrepreneurial discontinuous, based on expected futures	Creative discontinuous, based on creativity
Responsiveness Of organizational capability	Custodial	Production	Marketing	Strategic	Flexible
	Precedent-driven	Efficiency-Driven	Market-driven	Environment-driven	Seeks to create environment
	Suppresses Change	Adapts to change	Seeks familiar change operating	Seeks new change	Seeks novel change
	Seeks stability	Seeks	Seeks	strategic	Seeks creativity efficiency
	Closed system				Open system

Business and Technological Downstream Coupling

A number of Knowledge Management processes and mechanisms can be used to facilitate knowledge integration across business and IT. Two such processes are IT manager participation in business planning and business manager participation in strategic IT planning (Kearns and Lederer, 2003). Within the context of strategic IT planning, knowledge integration relates to the integration of business and IT knowledge. An important outcome of this knowledge integration is greater linkage of the strategic IT plan to business goals and objectives, with the focus on the extent to which the strategic IT plan is aligned with the business strategy. Thus it can be argued that knowledge context facilitates sharing of domain knowledge (the knowledge integration process), and this in turn affects knowledge integration outcomes (Reich and Benbasat, 1996, 2000 and Sabherwal, 1999).

The strategic business and technological alignment assess relevant insights from the knowledge-based theory and the resource-based view of the firm to conduct research through Knowledge Management processes, mechanisms and strategic dimensions of technology that can be used to facilitate knowledge integration across business and Information Technology. The following paragraphs address, on both business and IT managerial levels some of the functions considered in this study to achieve strategic alignment between business and IT.

Strategic priorities originate from the firm's vision and mission. As the business environment changes, strategic priorities will change. It is common practice in business firms to use two performance objectives: Growth performance and profit performance.

Goal setting is a key step to ensure that IT goals are aligned with the firm mission, objectives and strategic priorities. Innovative uses of emerging technologies such as Component Business Modeling and Services Oriented Architectures, coupled with an increased number of industry-specific standards, are delivering the tools and methods to bridge business and IT more easily and efficiently (Von Kanel, 2006). Information Technology Infrastructure Library and Control Objectives for Information and related technology are examples of industry-specific standards.

The impact of technology depends on the technological turbulence of the environment. The general management capability components that are impacted by technological variables such as product life cycles and the rate of technological change are: Involvement in innovation management, expertise in management of technology, innovative culture, firm flexibility, project management, strategic control, technological information system, and budgeting for innovation.

To understand cultural differences between the U.S. and Mexico, the innovative culture is addressed from a cross-cultural dimension. In the U.S., which is said to have weak uncertainty avoidance, there is less resistance to change, a willingness to take risks, less acceptance of rules and regulations, and a view of conflict as natural and inevitable. Alternatively, Mexico is characterized as having strong uncertainty avoidance, value conservatism, risk avoidance, security, and law and order through written rules and regulations.

One of the technological characteristics of environment that impact general management capability is the rate of technological change. Findings related to the implementation of technological change suggest that the adoption of technological changes by individuals is largely based on their perceptions of how the technology will impact their jobs. Consequently, it appears that individuals who perceive that technology changes will improve their ability to perform their job tasks may be more willing to adopt the technology (Schraeder et al., 2006).

Past research has assumed that decision makers accurately perceive environmental issues and formulate their strategies based on their own perceptions (Sutcliffe, 1994).

143

Individual judgments and perceptions of the involved managers are highly influenced by their personal strategic culture, personality, mindset, and prior experiences. For example, executive management tends to view the introduction of IT as an economic imperative while IT specialists tend to view it as a technical imperative.

There are three typical gaps confronted by general managers and technologists in turbulent, technology-intensive industries: (1) the information gap, in which knowledge workers are kept from contact with the strategists by several intervening layers of managers who have neither competence nor interest in technology and who suppress and filter technological information; (2) the semantic gap, consisting of differences in language, concepts, and perception of success factors between the general managers and the R&D managers; (3) the objectives/value gap, in which the technologist considers a technologically feasible advance as reason enough to go to the market, while the general managers need to be convinced of its potential profitability (Ansoff and McDonnell, 1990).

Five critical behavioral functions are identified within technology-based innovation activities in an R&D project. These functions are idea generating, entrepreneurship or championing, project leading, gatekeeping, and sponsoring or coaching. Each type must be recruited, managed and supported differently; offered different sets of incentives; and supervised with different types of measures and controls. Organizations have failed to be innovative solely because one or more of these five critical roles has been absent (Roberts and Fusfeld, 1982).

144

The Research Model

The research model depicted in Figure 21 shows a mechanism of how convergence could affect the overall Performance on Information Technology Convergence Issues and competitive advantage and how it could improve and complement the Strategic Success Hypothesis, considering other dimensions of IT responsiveness or technology aggressiveness to improve upon the concept of integrative management. That is, a firm's Performance on Information Technology Convergence Issues will be optimal when the information technology aggressiveness of the firm's strategic behavior matches the turbulence of its technological environment, the responsiveness of the firm's technology capability matches the aggressiveness of its strategy and the components of the firm's technology capability are supportive of one another.

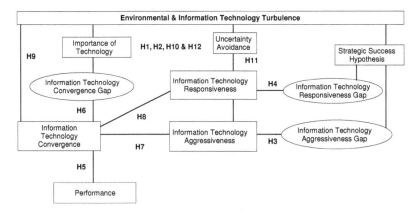

Figure 21

The Research Model

Research Variables

There are four independent variables: Information Technology Turbulence, Information Technology Aggressiveness, Information Technology Responsiveness and Information Technology Convergence. The last item is used in hypothesis 5, and is also a dependent variable in hypotheses 7 and 8.

The three intervening variables, calculated as "gaps," are the differences between Information Technology Turbulence, on one side, and Information Technology Aggressiveness, Information Technology Responsiveness, and Information Technology Convergence, respectively, on the other.

146

There are two independent variables: Performance on Information Technology Convergence Issues and Information Technology Convergence, to be used in hypotheses 7 and 8. The last item is also used as an independent variable in hypothesis 5.

Information Technology Turbulence

Information Technology Turbulence reflects the speed of change and instability of the technology environment and environmental turbulence reflects rapid market and technological changes that managers perceive as hostile and stressful conditions for their firm. Information Technology Turbulence is a combined measure of the discontinuity or changeability, predictability, and frequency of the shifts of the firm's environment. Information Technology Turbulence is measured on a 1 (low) to 5 (high) interval: (1) repetitive, (2) expanding, (3) changing, (4) discontinuous and (5) surprising. The level of Information Technology Turbulence is determined by the arithmetic mean of the answers from each individual respondent to four questions.

Information Technology Aggressiveness

Information Technology Aggressiveness is the firm's application of strategic technological tools, techniques, and know-how to position itself in the environment and shift executive thinking about technology convergence relative to the moves of competitors in its technological environment. Information Technology Aggressiveness is measured on a 1

147

(low) to 5 (high) interval: (1) stable, (2) reactive, (3) anticipatory, (4) entrepreneurial and (5) creative. The level of Information Technology Aggressiveness is determined by the arithmetic mean of the answers from each individual respondent to four questions.

Information Technology Responsiveness

Information Technology Responsiveness is defined as the propensity and ability of general management to engage in behavior that will optimize attainment of a firm's long-term objectives through Schumpeterian, continuous improvement, exploitation and exploration competencies, uncertainty avoidance culture and technology changes. Information Technology Responsiveness is measured on a 1 (low) to 5 (high) scale and is determined by the arithmetic mean of the answers from each individual respondent to eighteen questions divided into five parts: (1) six questions related to Schumpeterian Competencies; (2) five questions related to Continuous improvement competencies; (3) one question related to exploitation and exploration competencies; (4) three questions related to uncertainty avoidance culture; and (5) three questions related to technology change.

Information Technology Convergence

Information Technology Convergence is the degree of integration of voice, data, and video over common network facilities within the firm and their communication features ability to affect people's experience and their environment. Information Technology Convergence is measured on an ordinal scale from 1 (low) to 5 (high). Information Technology Convergence is determined by the arithmetic mean of the answers from each individual respondent to five questions.

Information Technology Aggressiveness Gap

Information Technology Aggressiveness Gap is the degree of misalignment between the Information Technology Aggressiveness of the firm and the Information Technology Turbulence. Information Technology Aggressiveness Gap is measured by the absolute difference between the scores of Information Technology Aggressiveness and Information Technology Turbulence for each respondent. The range of possible scores is from 0 to 4.

149

Information Technology Responsiveness Gap

Information Technology Responsiveness Gap is the degree of misalignment between the Information Technology Responsiveness of the firm and Information Technology Turbulence. Information Technology Responsiveness Gap is measured by the absolute difference between the scores of Information Technology Responsiveness and the Information Technology Turbulence for each respondent. The range of possible scores is from 0 to 4.

Information Technology Convergence Gap

Information Technology Convergence Gap is the degree of misalignment between the Information Technology Convergence of the firm and Information Technology Turbulence. Information Technology Convergence Gap is measured by the absolute difference between the scores of Information Technology Convergence and Information Technology Turbulence of each respondent. The range of possible scores is from 0 to 4.

Performance on Information Technology Convergence Issues

While success on Performance on Information Technology Convergence Issues needs many causes, failure may need only one. This item assesses firms' usage level of convergence and their performance on technological issues, including benefits, factors and goals. Performance on Information Technology Convergence Issues is determined by the arithmetic mean of the answers from each individual respondent to six questions using a 5-point numerical scale.

Research Questions and Hypotheses

This section details the research questions and hypotheses concerned with the relationships among environmental turbulence, information technology convergence, strategic innovation management and overall firm performance of corporate leaders and Information Technology managers of high tech clusters in the cross-border region (San Diego, U.S. - Baja California, Mexico).

Research Question 1: What are the differences between the technological competencies of Mexican and American Managers?

Hypothesis 1: The differences between the technological competencies of Mexican and American managers are:

1a. Mexican managers will score lower on Schumpeterian competencies than American managers.

1b. Mexican managers will score higher on continuous improvement competencies than American managers.

Research Question 2: What are the differences between the technology innovation focus of Mexican and American managers?

Hypothesis 2: The differences between the technology innovation focus of Mexican and American managers are:

2a. Mexican managers will score higher in utilizing and expanding technology innovation, where it is expected that extensions of existing technologies will prevail.

2b. Mexican managers will score lower in technology innovation as one of the critical determining factors, where inventions of new proliferating technologies are expected to emerge.

Research Question 3: What is the relationship between Information Technology Aggressiveness Gap and Performance on Information Technology Convergence Issues?

Hypothesis 3: There is a positive relationship between Information Technology Aggressiveness Gap and Performance on Information Technology Convergence Issues.

Research Question 4: What is the relationship between Information Technology Responsiveness Gap and Performance on Information Technology Convergence Issues?

Hypothesis 4: There is a positive relationship between Information Technology Responsiveness Gap and Performance on Information Technology Convergence Issues.

Research Question 5: What is the relationship between firms' usage level of convergence and their Performance on Information Technology Convergence Issues?

Hypothesis 5: There is a positive relationship between firms' usage level of convergence and their Performance on Information Technology Convergence Issues.

Research Question 6: What is the relationship between Information Technology Convergence Gap and Performance on Information Technology Convergence Issues?

Hypothesis 6: There is a positive relationship between Information Technology Convergence Gap and Performance on Information Technology Convergence Issues.

152

Research Question 7: What is the relationship between Information Technology Convergence and Information Technology Aggressiveness?

Hypothesis 7: There is a positive relationship between Information Technology Convergence and Information Technology Aggressiveness.

Research Question 8: What is the relationship between Information Technology Convergence and Information Technology Responsiveness?

Hypothesis 8: There is a positive relationship between Information Technology Convergence and Information Technology Responsiveness.

Research Question 9: What is the relationship between Information Technology Convergence and Information Technology Turbulence?

Hypothesis 9: There is a positive relationship between Information Technology Convergence and Information Technology Turbulence.

Research Question 10: What is the difference between the Information Technology Environment chosen by firms' strategy in the cross-border region?

Hypothesis 10: There is no difference between the Information Technology Environment chosen by firms' strategy in the cross-border region.

Research Question 11: What is the relationship between uncertainty avoidance and Information Technology Responsiveness?

Hypothesis 11: There is a direct relationship between uncertainty avoidance and Information Technology Responsiveness.

Research Question 12: What is the difference between individuals with high levels of involvement in planning technology changes and individuals with low levels of involvement?

Hypothesis 12: Individuals with high levels of involvement in planning technology changes will react more positively to the changes than individuals with low levels of involvement.

Research Strategy

The primary framework developed in this study is an extension of Ansoff's Strategic Success Hypothesis. The Strategic Success Hypothesis has been empirically tested in different settings. In all settings, the hypothesis was statistically sustained at 0.05 or better confidence level. However, this study also focused on relevant insights from the knowledge-based theory, and the resource-based view of the firm to conduct research through Knowledge Management processes, Schumpeterian and continuous improvement competencies and their role in the strategic process, and the effects of IT adoption and usage on organizational performance.

In this study, the Strategic Success Hypothesis extension, the knowledge-based theory insights, the resource-based view of the firm, Schumpeterian and continuous improvement competencies and the effects of IT adoption and usage on organizational performance are operationalized through four independent variables identified as Information Technology Turbulence, Information Technology Aggressiveness, Information Technology Responsiveness and Information Technology Convergence; three intervening variables identified as Information Technology Aggressiveness Gap, Information Technology

154

Responsiveness Gap and Information Technology Convergence Gap; and one dependent variable identified as Performance on Information Technology Convergence Issues.

The descriptive-correlational design was selected to determine the relationships among the vast array of variables.

Data Sources

The data sources were business organizations with computer and communication technology installed base (IT high tech clusters with middle-level managers and corporate leaders) in the cross-border region (San Diego, U.S. - Baja California, Mexico). For consistency purposes in both regions, the research targeted small and medium enterprise (SME) segments in both countries: small enterprises in the 50 to 99 employee range, and mid-sized enterprises with between 100 and 999 employees.

To increase the number of usable responses, the data collection followed different strategies in each country. A traditional mail-in survey (see Appendix A) was sent to middle-level managers and corporate leaders of SMEs in San Diego County, identified through the Harte-Hanks CI Technology database (http://www.hartehanksmi.com).

A survey (see Appendix B) was distributed to middle-level and corporate leaders of 224 SMEs in Mexico through colleagues of the researcher at (1) The National Chamber of Commerce for Electronics, Telecommunications and Information Technology, known as CANIETI (Camara Nacional de la Industria Electronica, de Telecomunicaciones y Technologias de la Informacion, http://www.canieti.org/); (2) the nonprofit Information

155

Technology & Software Cluster (Cluster de Tecnologias de Informacion y Software de Baja California, http://www.corporativovirtual.com/itbaja); (3) The Center for Scientific Research and Graduate Studies of Ensenada (Centro de Investigacion Cientifica y de Educacion Superior de Ensenada, CICESE, http://www.cicese.mx/); (4) The North Border College (El Colegio de la Frontera Norte, COLEF, http://www.colef.mx); and (5) The Autonomous University of Baja California (Universidad Autonoma de Baja California, UABC, http://www.uabc.mx).

The data collection process took place during the period July 19 through November 9, 2007. Seventy survey questionnaires were received, thirty-two from San Diego County (5.4 percent response rate) and thirty-eight from Baja California (16.9 percent response rate).

Research Instrument

A survey questionnaire was sent to middle-level (business) and corporate leaders of SMEs in the cross-border region (San Diego, U.S. - Baja California, Mexico). A cover letter was included, describing the purpose of the study, documents for consent and brief instructions for returning it. The survey questionnaire was translated into Spanish by the researcher and certified by a professional translator (see Appendix C). An attempt was made to contact middle-level managers and corporate leaders either by telephone or e-mail.

The survey questionnaire was developed to include all the independent and dependent variables. The variables measured by the research instrument are divided into 5 parts and each part is composed of a number of questions on 5-point Likert scales (1=low, 5=high) for

156

assessing Information Technology Turbulence, Information Technology Aggressiveness, Information Technology Responsiveness, Information Technology Convergence and Performance on Information Technology Convergence Issues.

Any question in which N/A for *not applicable* was checked or for which no answer was selected, was not included in the calculations. Therefore, no value for that question was added in the numerator of the equations above, and the value of the denominator was reduced once for each question answered N/A or not answered.

Methods for Establishing Validity and Reliability Test Results

Table 17 presents the statistical results of a reliability analysis of the variables using Cronbach's coefficient alpha (r).

Table 17

Cronbach's Coefficient Alpha of Variable-Question Relationships

Composite Variables	Questions	Number of items	Coefficient Alpha (r)
Information Technology Turbulence	1 – 4	4	≥ .5980
Information Technology Aggressiveness	5 – 8	4	≥ .6933
Information Technology Responsiveness	9 – 25	17	≥ .6788
Information Technology Convergence	26 – 30	5	≥ .8757
Performance on Information Technology Convergence issues	31 – 36	6	≥ .7876

Pilot testing was also conducted to support reliability. The survey questionnaire was pilot tested through researcher's acquaintances at various high tech organizations in Southern California, including AT&T, Qualcomm, Kyocera, and others, and at two research centers in Baja California: the Center for Scientific Research and Graduate Studies of Ensenada (Centro

158

de Investigacion Cientifica y de Educacion Superior de Ensenada, CICESE,

http://www.cicese.mx/) and The North Border College (El Colegio de la Frontera Norte,

COLEF, http://www.colef.mx).

The content validity requirement was met through intensive review by three

professors at Alliant International University: dissertation chairperson Dr. Alfred O. Lewis

and dissertation committee members Drs. Rachna Kumar and Ali Abu-Rahma.

Criterion-related validity is demonstrated by comparing the test scores with one or

more external variables considered to provide a direct measure of the characteristic or

behavior in question. This study employs various published research criteria for Information

Technology Aggressiveness, Information Technology Responsiveness and Information

Technology Convergence. To provide a direct measure of the characteristics, a gap analysis

was conducted to measure the degree of misalignment between these variables and

Information Technology Turbulence.

Term construct-related validity is evaluated by investigating what qualities a test

measures, that is, by determining the degree to which certain explanatory concepts or

constructs account for performance on the test. In this study, all variables were measured by

the sum of varied multiple questions to produce single scores: 4 questions for Information

Technology Turbulence, 4 questions for Information Technology Aggressiveness, 18

questions for Information Technology Responsiveness, 5 questions for Information

Technology Convergence, and 6 questions for Performance on Information Technology

Convergence Issues.

Data Analysis Methodology

Partial correlations were used to test the relationships among variables. Partial correlations provide a measure of correlation between two variables by removing or adjusting for the linear effects of one or more control variables.

Data analysis was accomplished using three methods: (1) the Pearson Product-Moment Correlation Coefficient r was used to examine the relationship between variables and to reveal the magnitude and direction of the relationship; (2) a zero order multiple regression was used to analyze the relative importance among the variables; and (3) a t test to determine a significant difference between two sample means. The significance of the statistical tests was determined using null hypotheses. For the purpose of this study, 5 percent is used as the threshold to assess statistical significance ($p < 0.05$).

Assumptions and Limitations

The respondents understood the wording of the survey questionnaire. The respondents gave honest answers to the best of their knowledge and ability. This study was limited to the research model presented in Figure 21 that is embedded in the Global Model presented in Figure 20. The samples were selected from corporate leaders and Information Technology managers in the cross-border region (San Diego, U.S. - Baja California, Mexico) organizations. Appendix D presents the values for the research variables calculated from the responses in each returned survey.

Research Findings

The results of all of the statistical analyses are summarized in Table 18. These are

followed by a discussion of the research findings.

Table 18

Summary of Statistical Results (N = 70)

	Research Hypothesis	r/t	p	Supported ?
	Hypotheses tested by t tests			
1a	Mexican managers will score lower on Schumpeterian competencies than American managers. *38 Baja California managers (mean=3.504) versus 32 San Diego County managers (mean = 3.694)*	-1.020	< 0.314	No
1b	Mexican managers will score higher on continuous improvement competencies than American managers. *38 Baja California managers (mean=3.750) versus 32 San Diego County managers (mean = 3.820)*	-0.400	< 0.691	No
2a	Mexican managers will score higher in utilizing and expanding technology innovation. *38 Baja California managers (mean=3.316) versus 32 San Diego County managers (mean = 3.125)*	0.761	< 0.449	No
2b	Mexican managers will score lower in technology innovation as one of the critical determining factors. *38 Baja California managers (mean=3.632) versus 32 San Diego County managers (mean = 2.062)*	2.062	< 0.043	Yes
10	There is no difference between the Information Technology Environment chosen by firms' strategy in the cross-border region. *38 Baja California managers (mean=3.388) versus 32 San Diego County managers (mean = 3.461)*	-0.500	< 0.622	Yes
	Hypotheses tested by correlation (Pearson's r)			
3	There is a positive relationship between IT Aggressiveness Gap and Performance on Information Technology Convergence Issues.	-0.101	< 0.408	No
4	There is a positive relationship between IT Responsiveness Gap and Performance on Information Technology Convergence Issues.	-0.037	< 0.761	No

161

5	There is a positive relationship between firms' usage level of convergence and their Performance on Information Technology Convergence Issues.	0.419	< 0.001	Yes
6	There is a positive relationship between IT Convergence Gap and Performance on Information Technology Convergence Issues.	-0.173	< 0.153	No
7	There is a positive relationship between IT Convergence and IT Aggressiveness.	0.333	< 0.005	Yes
8	There is a positive relationship between IT Convergence and IT Responsiveness.	0.425	< 0.001	Yes
9	There is a positive relationship between IT Convergence and IT Turbulence.	0.163	< 0.179	No
11	There is a direct relationship between uncertainty avoidance and IT Responsiveness.	0.747	< 0.001	Yes
12	Individuals with high levels of involvement in planning the technology changes will react more positively to the changes.	0.383	< 0.003	Yes
	Additional Statistical Results. Hypotheses tested by correlation (Pearson's r)			
13	There is a positive relationship between IT Turbulence and Performance on IT Convergence Issues.	0.233	< 0.053	Yes
14	There is a positive relationship between IT Aggressiveness and Performance on IT Convergence Issues.	0.373	< 0.001	Yes
15	There is a positive relationship between IT Responsiveness and Performance on IT Convergence Issues.	0.367	< 0.002	Yes

Discussion of the Findings

No significant differences between Mexican and American managers in technological competencies were found in hypothesis 1. Hypothesis 1a predicted that Mexican managers would score lower on Schumpeterian technological competencies. Hypothesis 1b predicted that Mexican managers would score higher on continuous improvement competencies. Neither hypothesis was supported. Hypothesis 2 analyzed differences between the innovative focus of Mexican and American managers. Hypothesis 2a predicted that Mexican managers would score higher in utilizing and expanding technology innovation. Hypothesis 2a was not supported. Hypothesis 2b predicted that Mexican managers would score lower in technology innovation as one of the critical determining factors. Hypothesis 2b was supported, but in favor of Mexican managers.

Hypotheses 3 and 4 predicted that Performance on Information Technology Convergence Issues would be higher when the Information Technology Aggressiveness and Responsiveness Gaps were lower. Neither hypothesis was supported. Hypotheses 5, 7 and 8 predicted that when firms' usage level of convergence increased, Performance on Information Technology Convergence Issues, Information Technology Aggressiveness and Information Technology Responsiveness would also increase. The results of these three hypotheses were significant at the 5 percent level or better. However, hypotheses 6 was not supported. Hypothesis 6 predicted that as the gap between Information Technology Convergence and Information Technology Turbulence increased, Performance on Information Technology Convergence Issues would decrease. Hypothesis 9 predicted that as Information Technology Turbulence increased, firms' usage level of convergence would increase. This hypothesis was not supported.

Hypothesis 10 predicted that there would be no difference between the Information Technology Environment chosen by firms' strategy in the cross-border region. Hypothesis 10 was supported. Hypothesis 11 predicted that as Information Technology Responsiveness increased, uncertainty avoidance would also increase. The results were significant at the 0.1 percent level. Hypothesis 12 predicted that individuals with high levels of involvement in planning technology changes would react more positively to the changes than individuals with low levels of involvement. Hypothesis 12 was supported.

Additional statistical analyses were performed to support the Strategic Success Hypothesis. Hypotheses 13 predicted that Performance on Information Technology Convergence Issues would increase as Information Technology Turbulence increased. Hypothesis 13 was marginally supported. Hypotheses 14 and 15 predicted that Performance on Information Technology Convergence Issues would increase as Information Technology Aggressiveness and Responsiveness increased respectively. The results were significant at the 5 percent level or better.

Conclusions

The results for hypothesis 1 indicated no differences between the technological Schumpeterian and continuous improvement competencies of Mexican and American managers. The innovation competencies of corporate leaders and Information Technology managers in the cross-border region are based on the radical growth of knowledge stock and generative learning. This leads to discontinuous changes in the activities of an organization through development of new technological or organizational abilities, based on the incremental growth of knowledge stock.

The results for hypothesis 2 indicated mixed results between the technological innovation focus of Mexican and American managers. On one hand the focus of corporate leaders and Information Technology managers in San Diego County firms is primarily in utilizing and expanding technology innovation, where it is expected that extensions of existing technologies will prevail. On the other, the focus of corporate leaders and Information Technology managers in Baja California organizations is one of the critical determining factors of firms' future success, where inventions of new proliferating technologies are expected to emerge.

The results for hypotheses 3, 4 and 6 indicated no relationship between Performance on Technology Convergence Issues and the intervening variables calculated as "gaps" (Information Technology Aggressiveness Gap, Information Technology Responsiveness Gap and Information Technology Convergence Gap). These results refer to the three typical gaps confronted by general managers and technologists in turbulent, technology-intensive industries: the information gap, the semantic gap, and the objectives/value gap. For the technologist, a technologically feasible advance is reason enough to go to market, while general managers need to be convinced of its potential profitability (Ansoff and McDonnell, 1990).

The results for hypotheses 3, 4 and 6 confirmed that Performance on Information Technology Convergence Issues is higher when "gaps" were lower. That is, as the gaps between Information Technology Aggressiveness, Responsiveness, Convergence and Information Technology Turbulence increased, Performance on Information Technology Convergence Issues decreased.

An SME is myopic if its perception of the environment is too limited to accurately sense the existing and future turbulence levels, leading to inaccurate performance potential expectations (Ansoff et al. 1993: 120). Myopic gaps depicted in Figure 21 show that as the

165

"gaps" between IT Aggressiveness, IT Responsiveness, IT Convergence and IT Turbulence increased, Performance on Information Technology Convergence Issues also increased, and as the gaps between IT Aggressiveness, IT Responsiveness, IT Convergence and IT Turbulence decreased, Performance on Information Technology Convergence Issues also decreased.

Once the 23 myopic gaps are removed from the survey responses received (N=70), the results of hypotheses 3, 4 and 6 are significant at the 5 percent level or better.

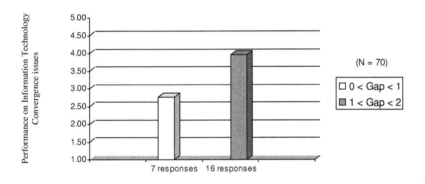

Information Technology Aggressiveness, Responsiveness and Convergence Gaps

Figure 22

Myopic Gaps

The results for hypothesis 5 indicated that Performance on Information Technology Convergence Issues was higher when firms' usage level of convergence increased. Furthermore, the results for hypotheses 7 and 8 indicated that firms' usage level of

166

convergence increased when the Information Technology Aggressiveness and the Information Technology Responsiveness of corporate leaders and Information Technology managers in the cross-border region were higher.

While the expectations of corporate leaders and Information Technology managers with respect to mobility and seamless interactivity are moving higher, it is evident that Information Technology Convergence is moving to a Transmit Control Protocol/Internet Protocol or TCP/IP backbone, a standards-approved Multiprotocol Label Switching (MPLS) connection-oriented networking technology in IP, and next-generation, or 4G, IP-based wireless technologies.

MPLS separates different customers' traffic from each other and supports individual customer virtual private networks. It also supports a mix of customer applications—such as voice, video and data—via appropriate quality of service metrics for multiple classes of service.

The Internet Protocol or IP makes possible converged wireless and wired services such as Web Digital Video Recorder remote control of home IPTV Systems. Furthermore, high tech companies are now deploying the next generation IPv6, which is expected to greatly expand IP addressing and accommodate the rapidly growing demand for devices and applications with Internet access over the next few years.

Although Global System for Mobile Communications (GSM) and Universal Mobile Telecommunications System (UMTS) with High Speed Packet Access (HSPA) technology has become one of the primary global mobile-broadband solutions, mobile operators continue with their mobile broadband evolution, aligning themselves with competing 4G technologies such as the Worldwide Interoperability for Microwave Access (WiMAX), Qualcomm's Ultra Mobile Broadband (UMB), or the Third Generation Partnership Project radio platform called Long Term Evolution (LTE) to download video to their phones, browse the Web faster than ever before and other data services that use up a lot of bandwidth.

The IP Multimedia Subsystem (IMS) is another key technology for Information Technology Convergence. It allows access to core services and applications via multiple-access networks. For example, during an interactive chat session, a user could launch a voice call. Or during a voice call, a user could suddenly establish a simultaneous video connection or start transferring files, while speaking to a customer-service representative.

With the projected increase in the use of mobile-broadband technologies, the amount of spectrum required by the next generation of wireless technology will increase too. Meanwhile, the Federal communications Commission (FCC) has scheduled auctions for the 700 MHz band in the United States to begin in 2008 (Rysavy Research, 2007).

Major companies have started championing open networks, where open access allows any device on any network, support of devices that run various open-source operating systems such as Linux, and download and use applications from any open source.

Open source means that the code is freely available and can be modified by users. For example, more than 30 companies have signed up for the Open Handset Alliance from Google, which aims to develop Android, a wide-open development environment for Internet access via mobile devices.

168

Open systems and cloud computing accelerate and foster the adoption of IT innovations such as how to build mobile Web applications that do not use a browser, but instead, rely on voice commands and speech-to-text translation to surf the Web.

The results for hypothesis 10 indicated no differences in the Information Technology Environment chosen by firms' strategy in the cross-border region.

The results for hypothesis 11 indicated a direct relationship between uncertainty avoidance and Information Technology Responsiveness of corporate leaders and Information Technology managers in the cross-border region with respect to their inherent impact on strategic thinking and behavior.

The results for hypothesis 12 indicated that corporate leaders and Information Technology managers in the cross-border region with high levels of involvement in planning technology changes will react more positively to the changes than individuals with low levels of involvement.

The results for hypotheses 13, 14 and 15 indicated that Performance on Information Technology Convergence Issues was higher when the IT Aggressiveness and the IT Responsiveness, respectively, were matched with IT Turbulence. These results supported the application of Ansoff's Strategic Success Hypothesis to the functional area of Information Technology Convergence in a cross-border region.

Since the 1980s, the Strategic Success Hypothesis has been empirically tested in different settings. In all of these settings, the hypothesis has been statistically sustained at a 0.05 or better confidence level. As a result, some researchers, including the committee members for this work, have suggested that the word "hypothesis" should be changed to something more appropriate.

Recommendations for Corporate Leaders and IT Managers

The study conclusions presented here suggest the following implications for practice.

1. The importance of corporate leader involvement in technology-based decisions in turbulent, technology-intensive industries, and hence the importance of bridging the three typical gaps confronted by IT managers: the information gap, the semantic gap, and the objectives/value gap. Both corporate leaders and Information Technology managers need to understand market trends such as globalization, virtualization and the mobile society. Globalization is driving growth, virtualization is driving customer demand for bandwidth and the mobile society is driving lower costs and seamless high network capacity, capable of delivering seamless high levels of interoperability and security.

2. The innovation focus of corporate leaders and Information Technology managers in San Diego County should be on the critical determining factors of firms' future success, where inventions of new proliferating technologies are expected to emerge. Both corporate leaders and Information Technology managers should focus on a revenue growth ramp – with substantial potential in wireless, business services, broadband, video and advertising.

3. Performance on Information Technology Convergence Issues is higher when firms' usage level of convergence increases. Some of the Information Technology Convergence variables that corporate leaders and Information Technology managers should

170

incorporate into their business model for the next generation of growth are differentiated mobility, seamless interactivity, increased functionality, scalability and low cost.

4. A firm's usage level of convergence increases when the levels of Information Technology Aggressiveness and Information Technology Responsiveness are higher. New technological capabilities and responsiveness will compel corporate leaders and Information Technology managers to explore new business opportunities in order to stay profitable in the long-term, using innovative service delivery strategies implemented through IT aggressiveness such as the Information Technology Infrastructure Library, Control Objectives for Information and related Technology, Capability Maturity Model Integration, and Six Sigma. If the budget permits, SMEs in the cross-border region are free to mix and match these frameworks rather than choose one over the other.

5. Corporate leaders and IT managers in the cross-border region with high levels of involvement in planning the technology changes will react more positively to the changes than individuals with low levels of involvement. For example, corporate leaders and IT managers with high levels of involvement could drive share and revenue growth, deploying seamless high speed data networks and new applications; boost demand for bandwidth; add seamless mobile voice to access high speed data; expand mobility applications; increase wireless penetration and drive incremental bandwidth.

6. When environmental turbulence associated with technological issues, innovative service delivery strategies implemented through strategic aggressiveness, and required responsiveness of organizational capability are aligned in an organization, performance on convergence issues is expected to be optimal.

171

Contributions to the Academic Field of Strategic Management

This study provided the following empirical evidence concerning:

1. The relationships among environmental turbulence associated with technological issues, innovative service delivery strategies implemented through strategic aggressiveness, required responsiveness of organizational capability and performance on Technology Convergence Issues. The results supported the application of Ansoff's Strategic Success "Hypothesis" to the functional area of Information Technology Convergence in a cross-border region.

2. Relevant insights from the knowledge-based theory and the resource-based view of the firm to conduct research through Knowledge Management processes. The Knowledge Management processes, mechanisms and strategic dimensions of technology can be used to facilitate knowledge integration across business and IT.

3. Innovation competencies compounded by two dimensions: Schumpeterian competencies and continuous improvement competencies.

4. Uncertainty avoidance and involvement in planning technology changes.

Contributions to the Practice of Strategic Management

This study has contributed the following to the practice of management:

1. Use of strategic innovation management and IT convergence strategies in SMEs in the cross-border region. (San Diego, U.S. - Baja California, Mexico.). Both corporate leaders

172

and IT Managers should focus on a revenue growth ramp – with substantial potential in wireless, business services, broadband, video and advertising.

2. Help for corporate leaders and Information Technology managers in the identification of convergence drivers for firms' future success to drive share and revenue growth, by deploying seamless data networks and new applications, boosting demand for bandwidth, adding seamless mobile voice to access high speed data, expanding mobility applications, increasing wireless penetration and driving incremental bandwidth.

3. In both high and low technology industries, the organization's technological innovation process is based on the radical growth of knowledge stock and generative learning. This leads to discontinuous changes in the activities of an organization through development of new technological or organizational abilities based on the incremental growth of knowledge stock.

4. The innovation focus of corporate leaders and Information Technology managers in the cross-border region. In San Diego County firms the focus is primarily on utilizing and expanding technology innovation. The focus in Baja California organizations is on the critical determining factors of firms' future success, where inventions of new proliferating technologies are expected to emerge.

Recommendations for Further Research

The following recommendations based on the findings and conclusions of this study are suggested for further research:

1. Conduct a study on the relationships between Performance on Information Technology Convergence Issues and the intervening variables calculated as "gaps" (Information Technology Aggressiveness Gap, Information Technology Responsiveness Gap and Information Technology Convergence Gap) differentiating between the responses of corporate leaders and Information Technology managers.

2. Further explore hypothesis 2b which predicted that Mexican managers would score lower than American managers in technology innovation as one of the critical determining factors, where inventions of new proliferating technologies are expected to emerge. Hypothesis 2b was supported in favor of Mexican managers.

3. Repeat this study in a variety of cross-border regions representing different technology environments, different innovation focus of managers and different organizational technological innovation processes.

4. Improve on the study by including additional variables to measure the latest Information Technology Convergence issues such as Open Systems, the IP Multimedia Subsystem and Service-Oriented Architecture.

5. This study included small and medium enterprises. It is recommended that this study be repeated and tailored for large firms and Strategic Business Units.

REFERENCES CITED

Abu-Rahma, Ali. 1999. "The relationships among national culture, strategic aggressiveness, capability and financial performance: The case of banks in Jordan and the United States." D.B.A. dissertation, United States International University, San Diego.

Ackermann et al. 1994. Using UNIX, Special Edition. Indianapolis: QUE.

Ahituv, N., and Giladi, R. 1993. Business Success and Information Technology: Are They Really Related? Proceedings of 7th Annual Conference of MIS, Tel Aviv University, Tel Aviv, Israel.

Alavi, M., and Leidner, D. 2001. "Knowledge Management and Knowledge Management Systems: Conceptual Foundations and Research Issues." MIS Quarterly 25, no. 1 (March):117-136.

Alpar, P., and Kim, M. A. 1990. "A microeconomic approach to the measurement of information technology value." Journal of Management Information Systems 7, no. 2, pp. 55-69.

Anand, Sandip, and Parashar, Vinayak. 2006. "Integrating Local and Global Knowledge through ICT: Implications for Rural Business and Development." IIMB Management Review (March).

Ansoff, H. Igor. 1972. "The Concept of Strategic Management." The Journal of Business Policy 2, no. 4, p. 3 from Khalil, T. 2000. Management of Technology. New York: McGraw Hill.

Ansoff, H. Igor. 1987. "The Emerging Paradigm of Strategic Behavior." Strategic Management Journal 8, pp. 501-515.

Ansoff, H.Igor, and McDonnell, Edward. 1990. Implanting Strategic Management Second Edition. New Jersey: Prentice Hall International.

Ansoff, H. Igor, et al. 1993. Empirical Support for a Paradigmic Theory of Strategic Success Behaviors of Environment Serving Organizations. Wiley & Sons.

Ansoff, H. Igor, and Antoniou, Peter. 2004. "Strategic Management of Technology." Technology Analysis & Strategic Management 16, no. 2 (June): 275-291.

Ansoff, H. Igor; Lewis, A.; and Antoniou, P. H. 2004. Strategic Management. XanEdu Original Works.

175

Argote, L; McEvily, B; and Reagans, R. 2003. "Managing Knowledge in Organizations: An Integrative Framework and Review of Emerging Themes." Management Science 49, no. 4 (April): 571-582.

Ataay, Aylin. 2006. "Information Technology Business Value: Effects of IT Usage on Labor Productivity." The Journal of American Academy of Business 9, no. 2 (September).

Athreye, Suma. 1998. "On Markets in Knowledge." Journal of Management and Governance 1: 232-253.

Barua, A; Kriebel, C. H; and Mukhopadhyay, T. 1995. "Information Technologies and Business Value: An Analytical and Empirical Investigation." Information Systems Research 6, no. 1, pp. 3-23.

Bedeian, Arthur. 1992. Management Laureates: A Collection of Autobiographical Essays by Igor Ansoff. Jai Press.

Benamati, S; Lederer, A. J; and Singh, M. 1997. "Changing Information Technology and Information Technology Management." Information and Management 31, pp. 275-288.

Biehl, Markus. 2007. "Success Factors for Implementing Global Information Systems." Communications of the ACM 50, no. 1 (January): 53-58.

Bright, J. R. 1969. "Some Management Lessons from Technological Innovation Research, Long Range Planning." pp. 36-41, from Martin, Michael J.C. 1994. Managing Innovation and Entrepreneurship in Technology Based Firms. New York: John Wiley & Sons.

Brynjolfsson, E. 1993. "The Productivity Paradox of IT: Review and Assessment." Communications of the ACM 36, no. 12, pp. 66-77.

Brynjolfsson, E., and Hitt, L. 1995. "Information Technology As a Factor of Production: The Role of Differences among Firms." Economics of Innovation and New Technology 3, no. 4, pp. 183-200.

Brynjolfsson, E., and Hitt, L. 1996. "Paradox Lost? Firm-level Evidence on the Return to IS." Management Science 42, no. 4, pp. 541-558.

Carrillo, Janice, and Gaimon, Cheryl. 2004. "Managing Knowledge-based Resource Capabilities under Uncertainty." Management Science 50, no. 11 (November): 1504-1518.

Chabane, H. 1987. "Restructuring and performance in Algerian state-owned enterprises: A strategic management study." Unpublished D.B.A. dissertation, United States International University, San Diego.

Chadwick, B. A., et al. 1984. Social Science Research Method. Englewood Cliffs, NJ: Prentice Hall.

Chandy, R. K., and Tellis, G. J. 1998. "Organizing for Radical Product Innovation: The Overlooked Role of Willingness to Cannibalize." Journal of Marketing Research 35, no. 44, pp. 474-487.

Christensen, Clayton. 1997. The Innovator's Dilemma: When New Technologies Cause Great Firms to Fail. Boston: Harvard Business School Press.

Cole, R. E. 1998. "Special Issue on Knowledge and the Firm – Introduction." California Management Review 40, no. 3, pp. 15-21.

Cooney, P. 2001. "The Mexican Crisis and the Maquiladora Boom." Latin American Perspectives 28, (September): 55-83.

Cronbach, L. J. 1960. Essentials of Psychology Testing, Second Edition. New York: Harper & Brothers.

Damanpour, F. 1996. "Organizational Complexity and Innovation: Developing and Testing Multiple Contingency Models." Management Science 42, no. 5, pp. 693-716.

Damanpour, F., and Gopalakrishnan, S. 2001. "The Dynamics of the Adoption of Product and Process Innovations in Organizations." Journal of Management Studies 38, no. 1, pp. 45-66.

Davenport, T. 1993. Process Innovation: Reengineering Work Through IT. Boston: Harvard Business School Press.

Davenport, T. H., and Beck, J. 2001. The Attention Economy: Understanding the New Currency of Business. Boston: Harvard Business School Press.

Davis, F. D. 1989. "Perceived Usefulness, Perceived Ease of Use, and User Acceptance of Information Technology." MIS Quarterly 13, no.5, pp. 319-339.

Day, George. 1994. "The Capabilities of Market-driven Organizations." Journal of Marketing 58, (October): 37-52.

DeLone, W. H. and McLean, E. R. 1992. "Information System Success: The Quest for the Dependent Variable." Information Systems Research 3, no. 1, pp. 60-95.

177

De Luca, Luigi, and Atuagene-Gima, Kwaku. 2007. "Market Knowledge Dimensions and Cross-functional Collaboration: Examining the Different Routes to Product Innovation Performance." Journal of Marketing 71, pp. 95-112.

Devaraj, S., and Kholi, R. 2003. "Performance Impacts of IT: Is Actual Usage the Missing Link?" Management Science 49, no. 3, pp. 273-289.

Dial, Gary. 2006. "New Carrier Business Models for Convergence." Lucent Technologies (June).

Dosi, F.; Teece, D. J; and Winter, S. 1992. "Towards a Theory of Corporate Coherence: Preliminary Remarks," from Dosi; F.; Riannetti, R.; and Toninelli, P. A. (Eds). Technology and Enterprise in a Historical Perspective. pp. 185-211. Oxford: Clarendon Press.

Drucker, Peter. 1994. "The Theory of Business." Harvard Business Review (September-October): 95-104.

Dyer, Nathan, and Kotlyar, Brian. 2007. "Anywhere Enterprise – Large: 2007 US Fixed-Mobile Convergence Survey." Yankee Group Research, Inc. (March).

Emory, C. William, and Cooper, Donald R. 1991. Business Research Methods. Homewood, IL: Irwin.

Feeny, Simon, and Rogers, Mark. 2003. "Innovation and Performance: Benchmarking Australian Firms." The Australian Economic Review 36, no. 3 (September): 253-64.

Fowler, Thomas B. 2005. "Convergence in Telecommunications: Meaning, History, Present Status, Future Rollout." Center for Telecommunications and Advanced Technology. (Retrieved June 24, 2005, from http://inet.intl.att.com/convergence/documents/Press/Convergence%20in%20Telecommu nications.pdf)

Freeman, Chris, and Soete, Luc. 2000. The Economics of Industrial Innovation. Cambridge, MA: The MIT Press.

Friedman, Thomas. 2006. The World Is Flat: A Brief History of the Twenty-First Century. Farrar, Straus and Giroux.

??Gibson, Jill, and Vestergaard. 2006. "Western Europe Fixed-Mobile Convergence Forecast 2005-2010." IDC #HP03N, vol. 1 (July).

Goldman, James. 1998. Applied Data Communications, A Business-oriented Approach. John Wiley & Sons.

Gopalakrishnan, S., and Damanpour, F. 1997. "Patterns of Generation and Adoption of Innovations in Organizations: Contingency Models of Innovation Attributes." Journal of Engineering and Technology Management 11, pp. 95-116.

Grant, R. M. 1996. "Toward a Knowledge-based Theory of the Firm." Strategic Management Journal 17, special issue, pp. 109-122.

Grossman, Martin. 2006. "An Overview of Knowledge Management Assessment Approaches." The Journal of American Academy of Business 8, no. 2 (March).

Gustafson Robert. 2003. "The relationships among environmental turbulence, strategic behavior, competitive (operating) behavior, and performance." D.B.A. dissertation, United States International University, San Diego.

Hair, Joseph F., et al. 2005. Multivariate Data Analysis, Sixth Edition. Upper Saddle River, NJ: Pearson/Prentice Hall.

Hanges, P. J; Dickson, M. W; and Lord, R. G. 1997. "Trends, Developments, and Gaps in Cross-cultural Research." Paper presented at the 12th annual conference of the Society of Industrial and Organizational Psychology, St. Louis, MO. (April).

Hart, Stuart, and London, T. 2005. "Developing Native Capability: What Multinational Corporations Can Learn from the Base of the Pyramid." Stanford Social Innovation Review.

Hatziantoniou, P. 1986. "The relationship of environmental turbulence, corporate strategic profile, and company performance." Unpublished D.B.A. dissertation. United States International University, San Diego.

Heldman, Peter K. 1998. Competitive Telecommunications. McGraw Hill.

Hitt, L. M., and Brynjolfsson, E. 1996. "Productivity, Business Profitability, and Consumer Surplus: Three Different Measures of Information Technology Value." MIS Quarterly 20, no. 2, pp. 121-141.

Hofstede, G. 1980. "Motivation, Leadership, and Organization: Do American Theories Apply Abroad?" Organizational Dynamics 9, no. 1, pp. 42-53.

Hofstede, G., et al. 1990. "Measuring Organizational Cultures: A Qualitative and Quantitative Study across Twenty Cases." Administrative Science Quarterly 35, pp. 286-316.

Holden, Nigel. 2001. "Knowledge Management: Raising the Spectre of the Cross-cultural Dimension." Knowledge and Process Management 8, no. 3, pp. 155-163.

179

Iansiti, Marco, and Richards, Gregory. 2006. "The Information Technology Ecosystem: Structure, Health, and Performance." The Antitrust Bulletin 51, no.1 (Spring).

Isaac, Stephen, and Michael, William. 1997. Handbook in Research and Education, Third Edition. San Diego: Educational and Industrial Testing Services.

Jaja, R. M. 1990. "Technology and banking: The implications of technology myopia on banking financial performance. A strategic management analysis." Unpublished D.B.A. dissertation, United States International University, San Diego.

Jaworski, Bernard, and Kohli, Ajay. 1993. "Market Orientation: Antecedents and Consequences." Journal of Marketing (January): 481-89.

Kahaner, L. 1996. Competitive Intelligence. New York: Simon & Schuster.

Kash, Don, and Rycroft, Robert. 2003. "To Manage Complex Innovation, Ask the Right Questions." Research – Technology Management (September – October): 30-33.

Kauffman, Robert, et al. 2006. "Systems Design, Process Performance, and Economic Outcomes in International Banking." Journal of Management Information Systems 23, no. 2, pp. 65-90.

Kauffman, R. J., and Kriebel, C. H. 1988. Modeling and Measuring the Business Value of Information Technology. Washington, DC: ICIT Press, pp. 97-119.

Keams, G. S., and Lederer, A. L. 2003. "A Resource-based View of Strategic IT Alignment: How Knowledge Sharing Creates Competitive Advantage." Decision Sciences 34, no. 1, pp. 1-29.

King, William. 2006. "Developing Global IT Capabilities." Information Systems Management (Fall).

Krafzig, D; Banke, K; and Slama, D. 2004. Enterprise SOA. Service-oriented Architecture Best Practices. Upper Saddle River, NJ: Prentice Hall.

Kulkarni, Uday; Ravindran, Sury; and Freeze, Ronald. 2006. "A Knowledge Management Success Model: Theoretical Development and Empirical Validation." Journal of Management Information Systems 23, no. 3, pp. 309-347.

Kumar, Rachna, and Kelly, Louise. 2006. "Self-Efficacy, Social and Cultural Issues in Designing Online Technology Skills Transfer Programs: A Mexican Context." Journal of Information Science and Technology 2, no. 4, pp. 72-92.

180

Laudon, Kenneth, and Laudon, Jane. 1998. Management Information Systems: New Approaches to Organization and Technology, Fifth Edition. Prentice Hall.

Lavie, Dovev. 2006. "Capability Reconfiguration: An Analysis of Incumbent Responses to Technological Change." Academy of Management Review 31, no. 1, pp. 153-174.

Lemelin, David. 2006. "Enterprise Business VoIP, IP VPN, and Convergence Adoption." In-Stat, SKUs: IN0603115SB, IN0603131MT and IN0603139EM. (December).

Lewis, A. 1989. "Strategic posture and financial performance of the banking industry in California: A strategic management study." Unpublished D.B.A. dissertation, United States International University, San Diego.

Lichtenberg, F. 1995. "The Output Contributions of Computer Equipment and Personnel: A Firm-Level Analysis." Journal of Economic Innovation and New Technology 3, pp. 201-207.

Lines, R. 2004. "Influence of Participation in Strategic Change: Resistance, Organizational Commitment and Change Goal Achievement." Journal of Change Management 4, pp. 193-115.

Loveman, G. W. 1994. An Assessment of the Productivity Impact of IT. Information Technology and the Corporation of the 1990s. New York: Oxford University Press.

MacDermott, Raymond. 2006. "Trade Agreements and the Environment: An Industry Level Study for NAFTA." Global Economy Journal 6, no. 3.

MacLaghant, C. 1998. "The Spirit of Systems Integration." Unisys (Retrieved October 10, 2005, from http://www.unisys.no/)

McDonagh, Joe, and Coghlan, David. 2006. "Information Technology and the Lure of Integrated Change: A Neglected Role for Organizational Development." Public Administration Quarterly. University of Dublin.

Mamaghani, Farrokh. 2006. "Impact of Information Technology on the Workforce of the Future: An Analysis." International Journal of Management 23, no. 4 (December).

Markides, Constantinos. 2006. "Disruptive Innovation: In Need of Better Theory." The Journal of Product Innovation Management 23, pp 19-25.

Markus, L. 2000. "Paradigm Shifts: E-Business and Business/Systems Integration." Communications of the Association for Information Systems 4, no. 10, pp. 1-44.

Marques, Daniel; Garrigos, Fernando; and Devece, Carlos. 2006. "The Effects of Innovation on Intellectual Capital: An Empirical Evaluation in the Biotechnology and Telecommunications Industries." International Journal of Innovation Management.

Martin, Michael J. C. 1994. Managing Innovation and Entrepreneurship in Technology Based Firms. New York: John Wiley & Sons.

Mendoza, Luis; Perez, Maria; and Griman, Anna. 2006. "Critical Success Factors for Managing Systems Integration." Information Systems Management (Spring).

Mirvis, P. H; Sales, A. L; and Hackett, E. J. 1991. "The Implementation and Adoption of New Technology in Organizations: The Impact on Work, People, and Culture." Human Resource Management 30, pp. 113-139.

Mitchell, Victoria. 2006. "Knowledge Integration and Information Technology Project Performance." MIS Quarterly 30, no. 4 (December): 919-939.

Narayanaswamy, Sathya, and Dhar, Rajive. 2002. "What's Preventing the Convergence of Voice and Data?" Lightwave Magazine, pp. 94-98.

Nonaka, I., and Takeuchi, H. 1995. The Knowledge-creating Company: How Japanese Companies Create the Dynamics of Innovation. New York: Oxford University Press.

Owens, Nathan, and Walshok, Mary. 2005. "Borderless Innovation." (Retrieved March 29, 2007, from http://www.sandiegodialogue.org/borderless.htm)

Patel, P., and Pavitt, K. 1994. "Technological Competencies in the World's Largest Firms: Characteristics, Constraints and Scope for Managerial Choice." STEEP Discussion Paper 13. Science Policy Research Unit, University of Sussex.

Pijpers, Guus, and Montfort, Kees. 2006. "An Investigation of Factors That Influence Senior Executives to Accept Innovations in Information Technology." International Journal of Management 23, no.1, (March): 11-23.

Polkinghorne, Donald. 1983. Methodology for the Human Sciences: Systems of Inquiry. Albany: State University of New York Press.

Prahalad, C. K. 1998. "Managing Discontinuities: The Emerging Challenges." Research Technology Management Journal (May-June): 14-22.

Reich, B. H., and Benbasat, I. 1996. "Measuring the Linkage Between Business and Information Technology Objectives." MIS Quarterly 20, no. 1, pp. 55-81.

Reich, B. H., and Benbasat, I. 2000. "Factors That Influence the Social Dimension of Alignment Between Business and IT Objectives." MIS Quarterly 24, no. 1, pp. 81-113.

Rigby, Darrel. 2005. "Management Tools 2005." Bain & Company (Retrieved March 29, 2007, from http://www.bain.com/management_tools/2005_tools_strategy_brief.pdf).

Roach, S. 1987. "America's Technology Dilemma: A Profile of the Information Economy." Special Economic Study, Morgan Stanley.

Roberts, Edward. 2007. "Managing Invention and Innovation." Research Technology Management Journal (January – February).

Roberts, E., and Fusfeld, Alan. 1982. Career Issues in Human Resource Management. Englewood Cliffs, NJ: Prentice-Hall, Inc.

Rosenberg. 1976. Perspectives on Technology. Cambridge University Press, from Athreye, Suma. 1998. "On Markets in Knowledge." Journal of Management and Governance 1, pp. 231-253.

Rungta, Sanjay, and Ben-Shalom, Omer. 2006. "Enterprise Converged Network – One Network for Voice, Video, Data and Wireless." Intel Technology Journal 10, no. 1.

Rysavy Research. 2007. "EDGE, HSPA and LTE - The Mobile Broadband Advantage." (September).

Sabherwal, Rajiv, and Kearns, Grover. 2007. "Strategic Alignment between Business and Information Technology: A Knowledge-Based View of Behaviors, Outcome, and Consequences." Journal of Management Information Systems 23, no. 3, pp. 129-162.

Sahal, D. 1985. "Technological Guideposts and Innovation Avenues." Research Policy 14, pp. 61-82.

Salameh, T. T. 1987. "Analysis and financial performance of the banking industry in United Arab Emirates: A strategic management study." Unpublished D.B.A. dissertation, United States International University, San Diego.

Schmidt, J. 2000. "Enabling Next-Generation Enterprises." EAI Journal 2, no. 7, pp. 74-80. (Retrieved October 10, 2005, from http://www.bjournal.com/)

Schoenfeldt, L. F., et al. 1976. "Content Validity Revisited: The Development of Content-oriented Test of Industrial Reading." Journal of Applied Psychology 61, pp. 581-588.

Schraeder, Mike; Swamidass, Paul; and Morrison, Rodger. 2006. "Employee Involvement, Attitudes and Reactions to Technology Changes." Journal of Leadership and Organizational Studies 12, no. 3, pp. 85-100.

Schumpeter, J. 1934. The Theory of Economic Development. Boston: Harvard University Press.

Schumpeter, J. 1942. Capitalism, Socialism, and Democracy. New York: Harper.

Scott, S. G., and Bruce, R.A. 1994. "Determinants of Innovative Behavior: A Path Model of Individual Innovation in the Workplace." Academy of Management Journal 37, no. 3, pp. 580-607.

Seeley, Rich. 2000. "The Business of Integration." EAI Journal 2, no. 1. (Retrieved October 10, 2005, from http://www.bjournal.com/).

Shannon, Claude. 1993. Collected Papers. IEEE Press ISBN 0-7803-0434-9.

Singh, Prakash, and Bernstein, Boaz. 2006. "Research in the Innovation Management Area: Lessons from Quality Management." Problems and Perspectives in Management 4, no. 2.

Spender, J. C. 1996. "Making Knowledge the Basis of a Dynamic Theory of the Firm." Strategic Management Journal, Special Issue 17, pp. 45-62.

Stretton, Alan. 2004. "The Implications of Convergence for Regulation of Electronic Communications." Organization for Economic Co-operation and Development. DSTI/ICCP/TISP(2003)5/FINAL. JT00167398. (July).

Strnadl, Christoph. 2006. "Aligning Business and IT: The Process-driven Architecture Model." Information Systems Management.

Studt, Tim. 2005. "Measuring Innovation: Gauging Your Organization's Success." R&D Magazine, February.

Subramanian, A., and Nilakanta, S. 1996. "Organizational Innovativeness: Exploring the Relationship Between Organizational Determinants of Innovation, Types of Innovations, and Measures of Organizational Performance." Omega, The International Journal of Management Science 24, no. 6, pp. 631-647.

Sullivan, P.A.1987. "The relationship between proportion of income derived from subsidy and strategic performance of a federal agency under the Commercial Activities Program." Unpublished D.B.A. dissertation, United States International University, San Diego.

Sullivan, P. 2001. Profiting from Intellectual Capital: Extracting Value from Innovation. San Francisco, CA: Jossey-Bass.

Sutcliffe, Kathleen N. 1994. "What Executives Notice: Accurate Perceptions in Top Management Teams." Academy of Management Journal 37, no. 5 (October).

Swamy, M. R. 2005. "Focus on Technology Change versus Productivity of Skilled and Unskilled Workers Through 'Organizational Revolution': Financial Management Appraisal of Labour Command Theory of Wage Differentials." Journal of Financial Management and Analysis 18, no. 1, pp. 61-69.

Tellis, G. J., and Golder, P. N. 2001. Will and Vision – How Latecomers Grow to Dominate Markets. New York: McGraw Hill.

Triandis, H. C. 1993. "The Contingency Model in Cross-Cultural Perspective." In M. M. Chemers and R. Ayman (Eds.), Leadership theory and research. San Diego, CA: Academic Press.

Tushman, M., and Anderson, P. 1986. "Technological Discontinuities and Organizational Environments." Administrative Science Quarterly 31, pp. 439-65.

Tushman, Michael, and Nelson, Richard. 1990. "Introduction: Technology, Organizations and Innovation." Administrative Science Quarterly 35, (March): 1-8.

Vanhaverbeke, Wim, and Peeters, Nico. 2005. "Embracing Innovation As Strategy: Corporate Venturing, Competence Building and Corporate Strategy Making." Creativity & Innovation Management Journal 14, no. 3.

Violino, Bob. 2005. "Best-Practices Library Gains Fans." InformationWeek Magazine. (Retrieved July 25, 2005, from URL: http://www.informationweek.com/story/showArticle.jhtml?articleID=166401916

Von Kanel, Jurg. 2006. "Technology Trends and Their Possible Implications on the Financial Services Industry." Economic Papers Special Edition (December): 80-87.

Von Tunzelmann, G. N. 1996. "Localized Technological Search and Multi-technology Companies." Mimeo, Science Policy Research Unit; University of Sussex, UK.

Weldon, K. 2007. "Convergence Distribution Models, Advisory Report." Current Analysis. (February).

Wen, Joseph and Shih, Stephen. 2006. "Strategic Information Technology Prioritization." Journal of Computer Information Systems (Summer).

Werlin, Herbert. 2004. "The Benefits of Globalization: Why More for South Korea Than Mexico?" International Journal of Public Administration 27, nos. 13 & 14, pp. 1031-1059.

Wernerfelt, B. 1984. "A Resource-based View of the Firm." Strategic Management Journal 5, 3, (April-June): 171-180.

Whitworth, Brian; Fjermestad, Jerry; and Mahinda, Edward. 2006. "The Web of System Performance." Communications of the ACM 49, no. 5 (May), pp. 93-99.

Yeung, A, et al. 1999. Organizational Learning Capability: Generating and Generalizing Ideas with Impact. Oxford: Oxford University Press.

Yoffie, David B. 1997. Competing in the Age of Digital Convergence. Boston: Harvard Business School Press.

Yum, Jihwan. 2000. "The relationships among environmental turbulence, strategic aggressiveness of information technology, organizational information technology capability, and organizational performance." D.B.A. dissertation, United States International University, San Diego.

Zahra, Shaker; Ireland, Duane; and Hitt, Michael. 2000. "International Expansion by New Venture Firms: Internal Diversity, Mode of Entry, Technological Learning and Performance." Academy of Management Journal 43, no. 5, pp. 925-950.

APPENDICES

APPENDIX A

QUESTIONNAIRE (ENGLISH)

A SURVEY OF INFORMATION TECHNOLOGY CONVERGENCE

For the purposes of this survey, a converged fixed and mobile service is one that enables the user to access a wide variety of communications, information, and/or entertainment services, with consistent quality of services regardless of the end terminal used, the underlying network over which those applications run, or the user's location.

We are looking for answers from middle-level and corporate leaders in business organizations with computer and communication technology installed base (IT high-tech clusters) in the cross-border region. The following questions relate to your firm during the last three (3) years from 2004-2006. If you wish to add comments or elaborate on any answer, please do so at the bottom of the last page.

Which <u>one</u> of the following best describes your role in your business organization?
- O I am an American middle-level manager and/or corporate leader.
- O I am a Mexican middle-level manager and/or corporate leader.
- O Other. Please specify: _____

For each of the following questions in this survey, please check only one item (1=low through 5=high).
If more than one choice seems relevant, please select the one that would apply to the more significant issues.

Which <u>one</u> of the following best describes the range of your organization's business interests?
- O Local only.
- O Domestic.
- O Crossborder (Baja California, México and San Diego County, USA).
- O Regional (such as Pacific Rim, NAFTA, ASEAN, or EU).
- O Global.

Which <u>one</u> of the following best describes the successive challenges which your firm encounters in the Technology environment?
- O Challenges are almost non-existent, dealing only with familiar challenges.
- O Challenges are slow and extrapolable from the past.
- O Challenges are fast and extrapolable from the past.
- O Challenges are new but predictable based on past experiences.
- O Challenges are new and unpredictable due to their novelty.

Which <u>one</u> of the following best describes the pace of technological changes in your industry?
- O Changes were generally much slower than my firm's ability to respond.
- O Changes were somewhat slower than my firm's ability to respond.
- O Changes were comparable to my firm's ability to respond.
- O Changes were generally faster than my firm's ability to respond.
- O Changes were usually much faster than my firm's ability to respond.

Which <u>one</u> of the following best describes the predictability of technological developments in your industry?
- O Developments are much slower and totally predictable.
- O Developments are somewhat slower and forecastable.
- O Developments are rapid but predictable.
- O Developments are generally faster and partially predictable.
- O Developments are usually much faster and totally unpredictable.

To what extent .....?
A score of 1 means *not at all*, 2 means *slightly*, 3 means *moderately*, 4 means *very much*, 5 means *extremely*

	1	2	3	4	5
Your primarily focus is utilizing and expanding technology innovation only, where it is expected that extensions of existing technologies will prevail?	O	O	O	O	O
Your primarily focus is technology innovation as one of the critical success factors, where inventions of new proliferating technologies are expected to emerge?	O	O	O	O	C

Which <u>one</u> of the following best describes your company position technologically in your industry?
- O No longer a factor or is not likely to have a presence in the next five years.
- O Behind in technology or likely to fall behind in the next five years.
- O Roughly even with world-best but not exclusively the strongest.
- O In the leading positions and is not in danger of losing this position.
- O Absolutely in the leading position and no other firms have the technology.

Which <u>one</u> of the following best describes the strength of your Influence preference for the Technology chosen in your company?
- O Not Important.
- O Slightly Important.
- O Important.

o Very Important.
o Absolutely Important.

To what extent are you …..?
A score of 1 means *not at all*, 2 means *slightly*, 3 means *moderately*, 4 means *very much*, 5 means *extremely*, and N/A means *not applicable*

	1	2	3	4	5	N/A
Aware of your competences in innovation, especially with respect to key technologies, and capability for getting rid of obsolete knowledge, stimulating in exchange the search for alternative innovations?	o	o	o	o	o	o
Able to innovate and gain competitiveness by broadening the portfolio of products and technologies, rather than responding to the requirements of demand or to competitive pressure?	o	o	o	o	o	o
Capable for using IT in order to improve information flow, develop the effective sharing of knowledge and foster communication between members of your firm?	o	o	o	o	o	o
Capable for obtaining information on the situation and progress in relevant science and technology through systems of technological vigilance?	o	o	o	o	o	o
Capable for developing incremental change in technological products and processes using tools such as ITIL or CobIT, etc.?	o	o	o	o	o	o
Capable for developing new technological products and processes?	o	o	o	o	o	o

To what degree do you …..
A score of 1 means *not at all*, 2 means *slightly*, 3 means *moderately*, 4 means *very much*, 5 means *extremely*, and N/A means *not applicable*

	1	2	3	4	5	N/A
Have commitment and ability to inspire acceptance of change in the firm, eliminating resistance to new ideas and the "sacred" nature of the dominant view?	o	o	o	o	o	o
Have preference for assigning resources focused on the exploitation and/or creation of opportunities as opposed to a preference for tradition?	o	o	o	o	o	o
Consider change as something natural and desirable, stimulating its employees continuously question the way things are done so it can be improved, to solve problems and to offer suggestions?	o	o	o	o	o	o
Support the training and development of your employees so that they incorporate new skills, especially those required for the success of the company?	o	o	o	o	o	o
Develop effective suitable training programmes so that the firm's base of technological knowledge enables it to communicate with organizations for the dissemination of innovation and technological transfer?	o	o	o	o	o	o

What product innovation factors does your firm consider to ensure better decisions about refining existing competencies and developing new ones?
A score of 1 means *not at all*, 2 means *slightly*, 3 means *moderately*, 4 means *very much*, 5 means *extremely*, and N/A means *not applicable*

	1	2	3	4	5	N/A
Upgraded current knowledge and skills for familiar products and technologies	o	o	o	o	o	o
Invested in enhancing skills in exploiting mature technologies that improve productivity of current innovation operations	o	o	o	o	o	o
Enhanced competencies in searching for solutions to customer problems that are near to existing solutions rather than completely new solutions	o	o	o	o	o	o
Upgraded skills in technological product development processes in which the firm already possesses significant experience	o	o	o	o	o	o
Strengthened knowledge and skills for projects that improve efficiency of existing innovation activities	o	o	o	o	o	o
Acquired manufacturing technologies and skills entirely new to the firm	o	o	o	o	o	o
Learned product development skills and processes (such as product design, prototyping new products, timing of new product introductions, and customizing products for local markets) entirely new to the industry	o	o	o	o	o	o
Acquired entirely new managerial and organizational skills that are important for technological innovation	o	o	o	o	o	o

Which one of the following best describes for how long do you think you will continue to work for your company?
o Two years at the most.
o From two to five years.
o More than five years.
o More than five years but I probably will leave before I retire.
o Until I retire.

Which <u>one</u> of the following best describes your level of involvement in planning technology changes in your company?
- O Low level of involvement.
- O High level of involvement.

To what degree do you .....
A score of 1 means *strongly disagree*, 2 means *disagree*, 3 means *neutral*, 4 means *agree*, 5 means *strongly agree*

	1	2	3	4	5
Think that company rules should not be broken – even if you think it is the company's best interest	O	O	O	O	O
Have job stress (feel nervous or tense)?	O	O	O	O	O
Have job satisfaction after technology changes are implemented?	O	O	O	O	O

Which <u>one</u> of the following system integration levels is your company using to improve process flow and focus on customer services?
- O Establishing a basic infrastructure for exchanging information between applications, although without any real business intelligence being linked to the infrastructure.
- O Using more advanced middleware tools to standardize and control the information exchange between applications.
- O Transition from sharing information between applications to managing the information flow between applications.
- O Achieving external integration by real-time business applications, the transformation of business processes, and new customer-focused structures for redefining the organization.
- O New tools that will be used for system integration, because innovative technologies are constantly appearing.

Which <u>one</u> of the following best describes your level of Fixed-Mobile Convergence awareness?
- O Not aware / never heard of technology.
- O Aware of technology and not interested in adopting in my company.
- O Aware of technology and considering adopting in my company.
- O Have tested or trailed this technology in my company.
- O Have deployed this technology in my company.

Which <u>one</u> of the following is the most important feature that would entice you to invest in Fixed-Mobile Convergence?
A score of 1 means *not at all*, 2 means *slightly*, 3 means *moderately*, 4 means *very much*, 5 means *extremely*, and N/A means *not applicable*

	1	2	3	4	5	N/A
Integrating employee mobile devices with the corporate telephony system	O	O	O	O	O	O
Flat rate and reduced rate mobile calling on campus/office (in building)	O	O	O	O	O	O
Providing integrated wired and wireless support	O	O	O	O	O	O
Flat rate and reduced rate international mobile calling and roaming	O	O	O	O	O	O
Removing and replacing on-premises PBX and desk phones with mobile devices	O	O	O	O	O	O
Providing a shared office and mobile voice calling plan	O	O	O	O	O	O
Mobile call logging/tracking using the PBX	O	O	O	O	O	O

Which <u>one</u> of the following statements best describes the top barrier to deploying a Fixed-Mobile Convergence solution?
A score of 1 means *not at all*, 2 means *slightly*, 3 means *moderately*, 4 means *very much*, 5 means *extremely*, and N/A means *not applicable*

	1	2	3	4	5	N/A
Cost of solution	O	O	O	O	O	O
Network security	O	O	O	O	O	O
Comfortable with current telephony solutions	O	O	O	O	O	O
Complexity of integration with existing applications or IT infrastructure	O	O	O	O	O	O
Device limitations	O	O	O	O	O	O
Enterprise infrastructure limitations	O	O	O	O	O	O
Unsure of who offers this solution	O	O	O	O	O	O
Lack of experienced vendors	O	O	O	O	O	O
Unproven technology	O	O	O	O	O	O
Not provided by service provider of choice	O	O	O	O	O	O

Which <u>one</u> of the following statements best describes your opinion of Fixed-Mobile Convergence?
A score of 1 means *not at all*, 2 means *slightly*, 3 means *moderately*, 4 means *very much*, 5 means *extremely*, and N/A means *not applicable*

	1	2	3	4	5	N/A
Nice to have but not a critical application on the IT/Networking roadmap	o	o	o	o	o	o
Important to improving workforce productivity	o	o	o	o	o	o
An important means to reduce monthly mobile communications costs	o	o	o	o	o	o
Too expensive to deploy	o	o	o	o	o	o
Do not understand it to assess technology viability	o	o	o	o	o	o
Over-hyped solution with few measurable results	o	o	o	o	o	o

How valuable are these benefits of network convergence to your business?
A score of 1 means *not at all*, 2 means *slightly*, 3 means *moderately*, 4 means *very much*, 5 means *extremely*, and N/A means *not applicable*

	1	2	3	4	5	N/A
Cost Savings	o	o	o	o	o	o
Support of remote workforce	o	o	o	o	o	o
Reduce number of network elements to manage	o	o	o	o	o	o
Support of mobile workforce	o	o	o	o	o	o
Effective technology that connects to the corporate network	o	o	o	o	o	o
Better customer service	o	o	o	o	o	o
Better collaboration with customers, suppliers and partners	o	o	o	o	o	o

What factors do you consider to accept IT convergence innovations?
A score of 1 means *not at all*, 2 means *slightly*, 3 means *moderately*, 4 means *very much*, 5 means *extremely*, and N/A means *not applicable*

	1	2	3	4	5	N/A
Accessibility	o	o	o	o	o	o
Implementation Process	o	o	o	o	o	o
User Interface	o	o	o	o	o	o
Perceived ease of use	o	o	o	o	o	o
Attitude toward use	o	o	o	o	o	o

What goals do you consider to evaluate IT convergence systems?
A score of 1 means *not at all*, 2 means *slightly*, 3 means *moderately*, 4 means *very much*, 5 means *extremely*, and N/A means *not applicable*

	1	2	3	4	5	N/A
Extendibility: Use outside component/data add-ins?	o	o	o	o	o	o
Security: Resist outside attack/take-over?	o	o	o	o	o	o
Flexibility: Predict/adapt to external changes?	o	o	o	o	o	o
Reliability: Avoid/recover from internal failure?	o	o	o	o	o	o
Functionality: What task functionality is required?	o	o	o	o	o	o
Usability: Conserve system/user effort or training?	o	o	o	o	o	o
Connectivity: Communicate/connect with other systems?	o	o	o	o	o	o
Privacy: Manage self-disclosure and privacy?	o	o	o	o	o	o

How would you rate your overall firm performance in terms of ..... ?
1 - Poor   2 – Below Average   3 - Average
4 - Good   5 - Excellent

	1	2	3	4	5
Information Technology Convergence?	o	o	o	o	o
Growth goals achieved?	o	o	o	o	o
Profit goals achieved?	o	o	o	o	o

Thank you very much for completing this survey. Please use this space to add comments or elaborate on any answer:

_____

_____

APPENDIX B

QUESTIONNAIRE (SPANISH)

UN CUESTIONARIO RELACIONADO CON LA CONVERGENCIA DE LAS TECNOLOGIAS DE LA INFORMACION

Para propósitos de éste cuestionario, un sistema de convergencia tecnológica Fija-Móvil permite al usuario acceder una gran variedad de servicios de comunicaciones, información, y/o entretenimiento, con una calidad consistente sin importar los dispositivos utilizados, el medio físico por los que se transmiten las aplicaciones, o la ubicación del usuario.

Estamos buscando respuestas de gerentes de nivel medio y líderes corporativos en empresas con base tecnológica de computadoras y sistemas de comunicaciones en la zona transfronteriza. Las siguientes preguntas están relacionadas con la empresa que Ud. ha laborado durante los últimos 3 años, del 2004 al 2006. Si desea agregar comentarios o elaborar cualquier respuesta, por favor hágalo al final de la última página.

Cual de las siguientes opciones mejor describe su función en la empresa?
- o Soy un Gerente de nivel medio o líder corporativo Estadounidense.
- o Soy un Gerente de nivel medio o líder corporativo Mexicano.
- o Otro. Favor de especificar:_____

Para cada pregunta en éste cuestionario, por favor seleccione solamente una opción (1=mínimo a 5=máximo). Si más de una selección parece relevante, por favor seleccione la opción que se aplica más significativamente.

Cual de las siguientes opciones mejor describe la zona de operaciones de su empresa?
- o Mercado Local solamente.
- o Mercado Doméstico.
- o Región Transfronteriza (Baja California, México y Condado de San Diego, EUA).
- o Regional (tal como Pacifico, TLC, ASEAN, o UE).
- o Global.

Cual de las siguientes opciones mejor describe los retos que su empresa encuentra en el ámbito tecnológico?
- o Los retos son casi inexistentes, nos enfrentamos a retos cotidianos solamente.
- o Los retos aparecen lentamente y son extrapolaciones del pasado.
- o Los retos aparecen rápido y son extrapolaciones del pasado.
- o Los retos son nuevos pero predicibles basados en experiencias previas.
- o Los retos son nuevos e impredecibles debido a su novedad.

Cual de las siguientes opciones mejor describe la rapidez de los cambios tecnológicos en la industria que opera?
- o Los cambios son generalmente más lentos que la habilidad de mi empresa para responder.
- o Los cambios son un poco más lentos que la habilidad de mi empresa para responder.
- o Los cambios son comparables con la habilidad de mi empresa para responder.
- o Los cambios son generalmente más rápidos que la habilidad de mi empresa para responder.
- o Los cambios son usualmente más rápidos que la habilidad de mi empresa para responder.

Cual de las siguientes opciones mejor describe la predictibilidad de avances tecnológicos en la industria que opera su empresa?
- o Los avances son demasiado lentos y totalmente predicibles.
- o Los avances son algo lentos y pronosticables.
- o Los avances son rápidos pero predicibles.
- o Los avances son generalmente rápidos y parcialmente predicibles.
- o Los avances son usualmente más rápidos y totalmente impredecibles.

A que nivel está Ud.....?
Una calificación de 1 significa *ningún interés*, 2 significa *algo*, 3 significa *moderadamente*, 4 significa *mucho*, 5 significa *extremadamente*

	1	2	3	4	5
Enfocado principalmente en utilizar y ampliar innovaciones tecnológicas solamente, donde se espera que prevalezcan extensiones de tecnologías existentes?	o	o	o	o	o
Enfocado principalmente en innovaciones tecnológicas como uno de los factores determinantes de éxito, donde es común que emerjan nuevas tecnologías?	o	o	o	o	o

Cual de las siguientes opciones mejor describe la posición tecnológica en la industria en que opera su empresa?
- o La posición no es un factor importante o no tendremos presencia en los siguientes cinco años.
- o Retrazados tecnológicamente o esperamos retrazarnos en los siguientes cinco años.
- o Estamos parejos con los mejores, pero no somos los más fuertes.
- o En una posición líder y no estamos en peligro de perder esa posición.
- o Absolutamente somos líder y ninguna otra empresa tiene la misma tecnología.

Cual de las siguientes opciones mejor describe su poder de influencia para seleccionar la tecnología en su empresa?
- o No es Importante.
- o Poco Importante.

o Importante.
o Muy Importante.
o Absolutamente Importante.

A que nivel está Ud…..?
Una calificación de 1 significa *ningún interés*, 2 significa *algo*, 3 significa *moderadamente*, 4 significa *mucho*, 5 significa *extremadamente*, y N/A significa *no aplicable*.

	1	2	3	4	5	N/A
Enterado de sus capacidades en innovación, especialmente con respecto a tecnologías de punta, y de su capacidad para deshacerse de conocimientos obsoletos, estimulado por la búsqueda de innovaciones alternas?	o	o	o	o	o	o
Capacitado para innovar y competir al ampliar su portafolio de productos y tecnologías, en vez de responder a los requerimientos de presiones competitivas de mercado?	o	o	o	o	o	o
Capacitado en el uso de tecnologías para mejorar el flujo de la Información, desarrollar mecanismos efectivos para compartir conocimiento y promover la comunicación entre miembros de su empresa?	o	o	o	o	o	o
Capacitado para obtener información acerca de la situación y progreso en ciencia y tecnologías relevantes a través de sistemas de monitoreo tecnológico?	o	o	o	o	o	o
Capacitado para desarrollar cambios incrementales en productos y procesos tecnológicos a través de herramientas como ITIL, CobIT, etc.?	o	o	o	o	o	o
Capacitado para desarrollar nuevos productos y procesos tecnológicos?	o	o	o	o	o	o

A que nivel Ud……
Una calificación de 1 significa *ningún interés*, 2 significa *algo*, 3 significa *moderadamente*, 4 significa *mucho*, 5 significa *extremadamente*, y N/A significa *no aplicable*.

	1	2	3	4	5	N/A
Está comprometido y capacitado para inspirar aceptación por el cambio en su empresa, eliminando la resistencia a nuevas ideas?	o	o	o	o	o	o
Tiene preferencia para asignar recursos enfocados en la explotación y/o creación de oportunidades, en comparación a la preferencia por tradición?	o	o	o	o	o	o
Considera el cambio como algo natural y deseable, estimulando a sus empleados(as) a cuestionar continuamente la manera en que se hacen las cosas con el propósito de mejorar, resolver problemas y ofrecer sugerencias?	o	o	o	o	o	o
Apoya la capacitación y desarrollo de sus empleados(as) para que incorporen nuevas habilidades, especialmente las requeridas para el éxito de su empresa?	o	o	o	o	o	o
Desarrolla programas de capacitación efectivos de modo que la base del conocimiento tecnológico de su empresa le permite la difusión y transferencia tecnológica con otras organizaciones?	o	o	o	o	o	o

En relación a innovación de productos tecnológicos, a que nivel considera que Ud. se ha preparado para asegurar una mejor toma de decisiones en relación a refinar sus capacidades actuales y desarrollar nuevas?
Una calificación de 1 significa *ningún interés*, 2 significa *algo*, 3 significa *moderadamente*, 4 significa *mucho*, 5 significa *extremadamente*, y N/A significa *no aplicable*.

	1	2	3	4	5	N/A
He aumentado mi conocimiento y habilidades en productos y tecnologías familiares	o	o	o	o	o	o
He invertido en mejorar mis habilidades en la explotación de tecnologías maduras que mejoran la productividad de las operaciones actuales en innovación.	o	o	o	o	o	o
He mejorado mis capacidades en la búsqueda de soluciones similares a las existentes, en vez de buscar soluciones completamente nuevas.	o	o	o	o	o	o
He mejorado mis habilidades en procesos de desarrollo de productos tecnológicos, en donde la empresa ya tiene significativa experiencia.	o	o	o	o	o	o
He aumentado mi conocimiento y habilidades en proyectos que mejoren la eficiencia de actividades existentes en innovación.	o	o	o	o	o	o
He adquirido tecnologías de manufactura y habilidades totalmente nuevas a la empresa	o	o	o	o	o	o
He aprendido habilidades de desarrollo de productos y procesos tecnológicos totalmente nuevos a la industria (tales como diseño de productos, prototipos, introducción de productos nuevos y mejorados al mercado).	o	o	o	o	o	o
He adquirido habilidades gerenciales y operacionales totalmente nuevas que son importantes para el proceso de innovación tecnológica.	o	o	o	o	o	o

Cual de las siguientes opciones mejor describe por cuanto tiempo continuará trabajando para ésta compañía?
o Dos años máximo.
o De dos a cinco años.
o Más de cinco años.
o Mas de cinco años, pero probablemente me saldré antes de retirarme.
o Hasta que me retire.

Cual de las siguientes opciones mejor describe su nivel de involucramiento en la planeación de cambios tecnológicos en su empresa?
o Mínimo nivel de involucramiento.
o Máximo nivel de involucramiento.

A que nivel Ud......
Una calificación de 1 significa *completamente en desacuerdo*, 2 significa *en desacuerdo*, 3 significa *neutral*, 4 significa *en acuerdo*, 5 significa *completamente en acuerdo*

	1	2	3	4	5
Piensa que las reglas de la compañía no deben romperse – aun si piensa que sea en el mejor interés de la empresa	o	o	o	o	o
Tiene stress laboral (se siente nervioso o tenso)?	o	o	o	o	o
Tiene satisfacción laboral después de que cambios tecnológicos se implementan?	o	o	o	o	o

Cual de las siguientes opciones mejor describe los niveles de integración de sistemas que su empresa utiliza para mejorar flujo de información y para enfocarse en mejorar servicios al cliente?
o Estableciendo una estructura básica para el intercambio de información entre aplicaciones, aunque sin ninguna inteligencia asociada a la infraestructura.
o Usando herramientas de middleware más avanzadas para estandarizar y controlar el intercambio de información entre aplicaciones.
o Transición de compartir información entre aplicaciones a manejar el flujo de información entre aplicaciones.
o Realizando integración externa a través de aplicaciones en tiempo-real, transformación de procesos, y nuevas estructuras enfocadas al cliente para redefinir la organización de la empresa.
o Nuevas herramientas que serán utilizadas para integración de sistemas, debido a que tecnologías innovadoras aparecen constantemente.

Cual de las siguientes opciones mejor describe su nivel de conocimiento de la convergencia tecnológica Fija-Móvil?
o No estoy enterado / nunca he escuchado acerca de ésta tecnología.
o Estoy enterado de la tecnología y no estoy interesado en adoptarla en mi empresa.
o Estoy enterado de la tecnología y estoy interesado en adoptarla en mi empresa.
o He intentado o hecho pruebas con esta tecnología en mi empresa.
o He implementado ésta tecnología en mi empresa.

A que nivel Ud. considera importantes las siguientes características para invertir en convergencia tecnológica Fija-Móvil? Una calificación de 1 significa *ningún interés*, 2 significa *algo*, 3 significa *moderadamente*, 4 significa *mucho*, 5 significa *extremadamente*, y N/A significa *no aplicable*.

	1	2	3	4	5	N/A
Integrar dispositivos móviles de los empleados con el sistema telefónico de la empresa	o	o	o	o	o	o
Tarifa fija y reducida por llamadas desde su dispositivo móvil en la oficina (edificio)	o	o	o	o	o	o
Provisión de soporte técnico integrado inalámbrico y alámbrico	o	o	o	o	o	o
Tarifa fija y reducida por llamadas internacionales/roaming desde su dispositivo móvil	o	o	o	o	o	o
Remover y reemplazar el conmutador telefónico (PBX) con dispositivos móviles	o	o	o	o	o	o
Provisión de oficinas compartidas y un plan de llamadas de telefonía móvil	o	o	o	o	o	o
Registro / seguimiento de llamadas móviles usando el PBX	o	o	o	o	o	o

A que nivel Ud. considera los siguientes obstáculos para la implementación de soluciones de convergencia tecnológica Fija-Móvil? Una calificación de 1 significa *ningún interés*, 2 significa *algo*, 3 significa *moderadamente*, 4 significa *mucho*, 5 significa *extremadamente*, y N/A significa *no aplicable*.

	1	2	3	4	5	N/A
Alto Costo de implementación	o	o	o	o	o	o
Seguridad de la Red	o	o	o	o	o	o
Comodidad con soluciones de telefonía actuales	o	o	o	o	o	o
Complejidad de integración con aplicaciones existentes o Infraestructura de TI	o	o	o	o	o	o
Limitaciones de Dispositivos ofrecidos en el Mercado	o	o	o	o	o	o
Limitaciones de la infraestructura de mi empresa	o	o	o	o	o	o
No estar seguro de que proveedor ofrece esta solución	o	o	o	o	o	o
Falta de proveedores con experiencia	o	o	o	o	o	o
Tecnología no establecida	o	o	o	o	o	o
No es ofrecida por mi proveedor de preferencia	o	o	o	o	o	o

De las siguientes opiniones, cual es el nivel que considerado por Ud. acerca de convergencia tecnológica Fija-Móvil?
Una calificación de 1 significa *ningún interés*, 2 significa *algo*, 3 significa *moderadamente*, 4 significa *mucho*, 5 significa *extremadamente*, y N/A significa *no aplicable.*

	1	2	3	4	5	N/A
Es bueno contar con ésta tecnología, pero no es una aplicación crítica en los planes del departamento de TI/Redes de mi empresa	o	o	o	o	o	o
Es importante para mejorar la productividad de mis empleados	o	o	o	o	o	o
Es un importante medio para reducir los costos mensuales por comunicaciones móviles	o	o	o	o	o	o
Es muy caro de implementar ésta tecnología	o	o	o	o	o	o
No entiendo la tecnología para determinar su viabilidad en mi empresa	o	o	o	o	o	o
Es una solución sobre-inflada, con pocos resultados mesurables	o	o	o	o	o	o

Acerca de los beneficios de convergencia tecnológica Fija-Móvil, cual es el nivel que Ud. considera de valor para su negocio?
Una calificación de 1 significa ningún interés, 2 significa algo, 3 significa moderadamente, 4 significa mucho, 5 significa extremadamente, y N/A significa no aplicable.

	1	2	3	4	5	N/A
Ahorro considerable	o	o	o	o	o	o
Apoyo a mis empleados que trabajan fuera del corporativo (de forma remota)	o	o	o	o	o	o
Reduce el numero de elementos a administrar en la red de datos	o	o	o	o	o	o
Apoyo de mis empleados para que tengan movilidad fuera de su oficina	o	o	o	o	o	o
Tecnología efectiva que permite conectarse a la red corporativa	o	o	o	o	o	o
Mejor servicio al cliente	o	o	o	o	o	o
Mejor colaboración con clientes, proveedores y socios	o	o	o	o	o	o

De los siguientes factores, a que nivel considera importante para que Ud. acepte innovaciones en la convergencia en Tecnologías de la Información?
Una calificación de 1 significa *ningún interés*, 2 significa *algo*, 3 significa *moderadamente*, 4 significa *mucho*, 5 significa *extremadamente*, y N/A significa *no aplicable.*

	1	2	3	4	5	N/A
Accesibilidad	o	o	o	o	o	o
Proceso de Implementación	o	o	o	o	o	o
Interfaz con el Usuario	o	o	o	o	o	o
Percepción en la Facilidad de utilización	o	o	o	o	o	o
Actitud hacia la utilización	o	o	o	o	o	o

De los siguientes factores, a que nivel Ud. considera importante en la evaluación sistemas de convergencia en Tecnologías de la Información? Una calificación de 1 significa *ningún interés*, 2 significa *algo*, 3 significa *moderadamente*, 4 significa *mucho*, 5 significa *extremadamente*, y N/A significa *no aplicable.*

	1	2	3	4	5	N/A
Extensibilidad: Usar componentes externos/módulos?	o	o	o	o	o	o
Seguridad: Contrarrestar ataques/invasiones externas?	o	o	o	o	o	o
Flexibilidad: Predecir/Adaptarse a cambios externos?	o	o	o	o	o	o
Confiabilidad: Evitar/Recuperarse de fallas internas?	o	o	o	o	o	o
Funcionalidad: Que tarea/función es requerida?	o	o	o	o	o	o
Usabilidad: Conservar sistema/usuario o entrenamiento?	o	o	o	o	o	o
Conectividad: Comunicar/conectar con otros sistemas?	o	o	o	o	o	o
Privacidad: Administrar aislamiento y privacidad?	o	o	o	o	o	o

Como calificaría el rendimiento total de su empresa en términos de ..... ?
1 – Pobre. 2 – Debajo del Promedio. 3 - Promedio.
4 – Sobre el Promedio. 5 – Excelente.

	1	2	3	4	5
Convergencia en Tecnologías de la Información?	o	o	o	o	o
Objetivos de crecimiento alcanzados?	o	o	o	o	o
Objetivos de ganancias netas alcanzados?	o	o	o	o	o

Favor de utilizar éste espacio para agregar comentarios o elaborar cualquier respuesta:

_____

_____

APPENDIX C

CALCULATED VARIABLES

Notes:
- Baja California responses are shown in shaded
- High Level of involvement in technology changes are shown in **bold**
- IT = Information Technology

Response Number	1	2	3	4	5	6	7	8	9	10	11	12
IT Turbulence	4.25	3.00	3.25	3.25	2.75	3.75	3.75	3.25	3.25	3.25	3.50	3.50
IT Aggressiveness	3.00	3.00	2.25	4.50	4.00	3.50	3.75	3.67	2.75	3.00	4.00	3.50
IT Responsiveness	3.22	2.90	3.08	4.17	4.30	3.73	3.50	3.47	3.87	3.90	4.23	3.59
IT Convergence	2.03	1.91	2.33	2.00	3.55	4.00	3.22	3.29	3.00	3.01	3.93	3.81
IT Aggressiveness Gap	1.25	0.00	1.00	1.25	1.25	0.25	0.00	0.42	0.50	0.25	0.50	0.00
IT Responsiveness Gap	1.03	0.11	0.17	0.92	1.55	0.02	0.25	0.22	0.62	0.65	0.73	0.09
IT Convergence Gap	2.22	1.09	0.92	1.25	0.80	0.25	0.53	0.04	0.25	0.24	0.43	0.31
Performance on IT Convergence Issues	2.84	3.01	3.46	3.67	3.81	4.00	3.28	3.38	3.70	3.07	3.36	4.28
Schumpeterian technological competences	3.00	2.67	2.67	5.00	5.00	4.00	3.33	4.17	3.50	4.33	4.33	2.67
Continuous Improvement competences	1.80	3.60	3.40	4.50	4.40	4.00	3.00	4.20	3.80	4.00	4.80	4.20
Utilizing and expanding technology innovation	4.00	3.00	3.00	5.00	4.00	4.00	3.00	3.00	2.00	3.00	3.00	5.00
Innovation as one of the critical determining factors	3.00	1.00	2.00	5.00	4.00	4.00	4.00	0.00	3.00	5.00	5.00	2.00
Uncertainty Avoidance Culture	4.33	2.33	3.33	3.67	3.33	3.33	3.67	2.33	4.33	3.33	4.00	3.67
Job Satisfaction after technology changes	**4.00**	**4.00**	**3.00**	**5.00**	**5.00**	**4.00**	**4.00**	**4.00**	4.00	4.00	**5.00**	**4.00**

Response Number	13	14	15	16	17	18	19	20	21	22	23	24
IT Turbulence	3.75	2.75	2.75	4.00	3.50	3.75	3.50	4.00	2.50	4.50	3.75	3.50
IT Aggressiveness	2.75	4.00	3.00	2.25	2.75	3.25	3.75	4.00	3.50	3.00	3.75	3.25
IT Responsiveness	3.83	3.49	2.92	3.52	3.19	2.49	3.78	3.85	4.44	4.31	4.04	3.43
IT Convergence	3.59	3.61	3.36	2.20	3.10	2.80	3.41	3.81	3.15	3.44	3.95	2.50
IT Aggressiveness Gap	1.00	1.25	0.25	1.75	0.75	0.50	0.25	0.00	1.00	1.50	0.00	0.25
IT Responsiveness Gap	0.08	0.74	0.17	0.48	0.32	1.27	0.28	0.15	1.94	0.19	0.29	0.07
IT Convergence Gap	0.16	0.86	0.61	1.80	0.40	0.95	0.09	0.19	0.65	1.06	0.20	1.00
Performance on IT Convergence Issues	4.39	4.11	3.02	3.10	3.45	2.83	2.94	3.46	3.84	3.01	4.24	2.97
Schumpeterian technological competences	3.83	5.00	3.50	2.50	2.50	3.50	4.83	3.83	4.67	4.00	4.67	3.60
Continuous Improvement competences	4.20	4.20	3.40	3.00	2.80	4.80	4.20	3.80	4.40	4.20	4.60	4.00
Utilizing and expanding technology innovation	2.00	4.00	3.00	2.00	4.00	3.00	5.00	4.00	3.00	3.00	2.00	4.00
Innovation as one of the critical determining factors	4.00	4.00	2.00	2.00	2.00	4.00	3.00	4.00	3.00	3.00	5.00	3.00
Uncertainty Avoidance Culture	3.67	2.00	2.00	4.33	3.33	0.00	2.67	4.00	4.33	4.67	3.33	3.33
Job Satisfaction after technology changes	**5.00**	3.00	**3.00**	**5.00**	**4.00**	0.00	**5.00**	4.00	**5.00**	**5.00**	4.00	4.00

Response Number	25	26	27	28	29	30	31	32	33	34	35	36
IT Turbulence	3.50	4.25	4.75	4.00	1.75	3.50	2.25	3.50	4.00	3.75	4.25	3.50
IT Aggressiveness	2.75	3.50	3.67	3.50	3.25	3.75	2.75	3.50	4.00	3.75	2.50	3.25
IT Responsiveness	3.38	4.02	4.13	3.10	3.26	3.29	2.64	2.34	3.78	3.75	3.08	3.75
IT Convergence	3.23	3.50	4.16	2.71	3.45	3.17	2.86	3.64	4.14	4.00	3.31	3.33
IT Aggressiveness Gap	0.75	0.75	1.08	0.50	1.50	0.25	0.50	0.00	0.00	0.00	1.75	0.25
IT Responsiveness Gap	0.13	0.23	0.63	0.90	1.51	0.21	0.39	1.16	0.22	0.00	1.17	0.25
IT Convergence Gap	0.27	0.75	0.59	1.29	1.70	0.33	0.61	0.14	0.14	0.25	0.94	0.17
Performance on IT Convergence Issues	3.31	3.97	4.24	3.60	3.52	2.39	3.01	3.90	4.36	3.95	3.18	3.75
Schumpeterian technological competences	3.50	3.83	3.67	3.50	3.33	3.50	2.00	3.67	4.17	3.83	2.60	3.83
Continuous Improvement competences	4.00	5.00	5.00	2.33	3.75	3.60	4.00	4.80	4.40	4.20	3.80	3.40
Utilizing and expanding technology innovation	2.00	5.00	0.00	4.00	4.00	4.00	3.00	2.00	4.00	4.00	2.00	4.00
Innovation as one of the critical determining factors	2.00	5.00	4.00	4.00	3.00	5.00	3.00	4.00	5.00	5.00	2.00	3.00
Uncertainty Avoidance Culture	3.00	3.00	3.67	3.00	2.67	2.67	1.00	0.00	3.33	3.00	3.33	3.67
Job Satisfaction after technology changes	**4.00**	**5.00**	4.00	**5.00**	**3.00**	4.00	5.00	0.00	**4.00**	5.00	4.00	**5.00**

Response Number	37	38	39	40	41	42	43	44	45	46	47	48
IT Turbulence	4.00	2.75	3.75	3.75	3.75	3.75	4.50	3.00	2.75	3.50	3.25	1.75
IT Aggressiveness	4.75	2.25	3.25	2.25	3.25	2.75	5.00	2.50	3.50	3.75	3.50	2.75
IT Responsiveness	4.35	3.62	2.76	3.58	2.76	2.58	3.97	3.05	3.59	3.59	3.17	3.38
IT Convergence	4.19	2.67	2.56	3.88	2.56	1.50	3.00	3.20	2.67	2.97	3.06	2.15
IT Aggressiveness Gap	0.75	0.50	0.50	1.50	0.50	1.00	0.50	0.50	0.75	0.25	0.25	1.00
IT Responsiveness Gap	0.35	0.87	0.99	0.17	0.99	1.17	0.53	0.05	0.84	0.09	0.09	1.63
IT Convergence Gap	0.19	0.08	1.19	0.13	1.19	2.25	1.50	0.20	0.08	0.53	0.19	0.40
Performance on IT Convergence Issues	3.96	3.67	3.29	4.03	3.29	3.40	4.50	2.60	3.86	4.05	3.11	3.18
Schumpeterian technological competences	4.83	2.50	2.83	2.83	2.83	2.50	4.25	2.00	3.60	3.80	5.00	3.17
Continuous Improvement competences	4.60	4.00	4.00	3.60	4.00	3.40	4.60	3.80	4.00	3.75	2.20	3.00
Utilizing and expanding technology innovation	5.00	1.00	3.00	3.00	3.00	3.00	5.00	4.00	4.00	4.00	3.00	3.00
Innovation as one of the critical determining factors	5.00	1.00	2.00	1.00	2.00	4.00	0.00	1.00	3.00	4.00	4.00	3.00
Uncertainty Avoidance Culture	3.67	4.33	1.67	4.33	1.67	2.00	3.00	3.00	3.00	3.67	2.67	3.33
Job Satisfaction after technology changes	**5.00**	3.00	**4.00**	3.00	**4.00**	3.00	3.00	4.00	**4.00**	2.00	**4.00**	**5.00**

Response Number	49	50	51	52	53	54	55	56	57	58	59	60
IT Turbulence	3.75	3.25	2.00	3.75	2.50	2.25	4.00	2.75	2.50	4.25	4.25	3.50
IT Aggressiveness	3.50	3.00	2.75	4.00	2.67	2.50	3.67	2.25	2.00	3.25	4.00	2.50
IT Responsiveness	3.18	3.88	3.64	3.04	2.93	3.33	3.07	2.83	2.71	3.10	3.80	2.41
IT Convergence	1.80	3.10	3.39	2.01	3.24	3.16	3.13	2.44	2.88	3.13	4.04	2.85
IT Aggressiveness Gap	0.25	0.25	0.75	0.25	0.17	0.25	0.33	0.50	0.50	1.00	0.25	1.00
IT Responsiveness Gap	0.57	0.63	1.64	0.72	0.43	1.08	0.93	0.08	0.21	1.16	0.46	1.09
IT Convergence Gap	1.95	0.15	1.39	1.74	0.74	0.91	0.87	0.31	0.38	1.12	0.21	0.65
Performance on IT Convergence Issues	3.38	3.42	3.18	2.98	3.41	3.86	4.05	2.66	3.14	3.66	3.99	3.53
Schumpeterian technological competences	3.20	3.17	3.83	2.83	4.17	3.50	3.20	2.80	2.50	2.80	4.33	2.40
Continuous Improvement competences	3.20	3.80	4.60	2.80	2.40	3.40	2.50	3.20	3.20	3.80	4.60	3.25
Utilizing and expanding technology innovation	3.00	4.00	4.00	4.00	5.00	3.00	0.00	3.00	2.00	3.00	4.00	3.00
Innovation as one of the critical determining factors	4.00	4.00	4.00	5.00	0.00	4.00	5.00	2.00	3.00	4.00	5.00	2.00
IT Environment chosen by firm's strategy	3.75	3.25	2.00	3.75	2.50	2.25	4.00	2.75	2.50	4.25	4.25	3.50
Uncertainty Avoidance Culture	3.00	3.67	3.00	3.00	2.00	2.33	3.67	2.00	2.33	2.67	2.67	2.00
Job Satisfaction after technology changes	4.00	4.00	4.00	5.00	4.00	5.00	5.00	4.00	4.00	4.00	4.00	4.00

Response Number	61	62	63	64	65	66	67	68	69	70
IT Turbulence	3.25	3.75	3.50	3.25	3.50	3.50	3.25	3.25	3.50	3.50
IT Aggressiveness	2.00	3.75	3.25	3.00	3.75	3.25	3.00	3.50	3.75	3.00
IT Responsiveness	2.48	3.44	3.03	3.31	3.57	4.00	4.07	4.37	4.13	3.50
IT Convergence	2.47	3.97	2.27	3.90	2.82	2.84	1.33	4.21	4.00	2.95
IT Aggressiveness Gap	1.25	0.00	0.25	0.25	0.25	0.25	0.25	0.25	0.25	0.50
IT Responsiveness Gap	0.77	0.31	0.47	0.06	0.07	0.50	0.82	1.12	0.63	0.00
IT Convergence Gap	0.78	0.22	1.23	0.65	0.68	0.66	1.92	0.96	0.50	0.55
Performance on IT Convergence Issues	3.28	4.16	5.00	3.80	3.53	3.66	3.34	3.76	4.08	4.02
Schumpeterian technological competences	3.50	3.80	4.20	3.67	4.20	4.67	3.50	4.60	4.00	3.83
Continuous Improvement competences	1.33	4.00	4.25	3.80	3.50	4.00	4.40	4.60	4.00	3.60
Utilizing and expanding technology innovation	2.00	4.00	3.00	3.00	3.00	2.00	3.00	2.00	3.00	3.00
Innovation as one of the critical determining factors	0.00	5.00	4.00	3.00	5.00	5.00	4.00	5.00	4.00	3.00
Uncertainty Avoidance Culture	2.33	2.67	1.67	2.33	3.00	4.00	4.00	4.00	4.33	3.00
Job Satisfaction after technology changes	3.00	4.00	3.00	4.00	4.00	3.00	5.00	5.00	5.00	4.00

www.ingramcontent.com/pod-product-compliance
Lightning Source LLC
Chambersburg PA
CBHW071426050326
40689CB00010B/2000